Praise for *Beat Gen*

'Everyone knows about the causes and consequences of gender bias, but few know how to combat it. This book, packed with practical suggestions, is a must-read for anyone interested in reducing gender bias and creating an inclusive workplace.'

Dr Tomas Chamorro-Premuzic, Chief Talent Scientist at Manpower Group, Professor of Business Psychology at Columbia University and UCL

'Dr Morley has extensive experience working with organisations and their leaders. Her insights, combined with her extensive knowledge of organisational behaviours, have clearly been brought to the fore in *Beat Gender Bias*. It is a very approachable and well-organised tool to enable anyone to understand bias, the situations that arise when bias is viewed as acceptable, and how you can turn a toxic environment into an inclusive one. I would recommend the book to anyone that is hoping to lead an organisation to maximise everyone's talents and create a highly productive organisation that will be successful into the future.'

Anthea Hancocks, CEO, Scanlon Foundation

'Creating a truly inclusive workplace, where your team genuinely want to put down roots and grow, starts with a mindset and culture of safety, connection and feeling welcome. A constant threat to this flourishing is bias, and as leaders it's often the unconscious thoughts that play out in the lived reality.

'*Beat Gender Bias* is a fantastic framework for raising awareness and identifying behaviours in ourselves and our teammates, and for challenging this head on in a way that brings teams on the right journey to a place of work that bears out the true nature of diversity and inclusion.'

Michael Schneider, Managing Director, Bunnings

'When organisations have a role to serve the community, naturally half the population benefiting should be women and girls. However, many studies demonstrate that there is unconscious bias in service delivery by government agencies. The tools and tips outlined in Dr Karen Morley's book *Beat Gender Bias* will assist councils to be more inclusive in service delivery to everyone across the community. Reading this will assist public sector leaders to make the invisible visible and then work to address equitable delivery of service.'

Ruth McGowan, OAM, Local Government consultant and trainer

'I have long been a believer in the critical importance of diversity of thought in achieving high performance. The GFC and economic cycles have seen many organisations without sufficient diversity of thought struggle or even disappear. Encouraging inclusion and listening are keys to leveraging the diversity dividend. How to successfully and consistently promote diversity and achieve inclusion are the hard parts. Thankfully, Karen's book gives all leaders the tools we need to do this.

'I was fortunate to have exposures to some amazing Male Champions of Change (MCCs) in my time at Aurecon. MCC leaders like Giam Swiegers and Bill Cox have highlighted the correlation between diversity and innovation as not being a coincidence – diversity drives innovation. The numerous industry awards won by Aurecon are proof of that. Not to mention that truly diverse and inclusive organisations are more fun to work in! With Karen's book in hand, I am confident many more leaders will be able to champion change and beat bias, to ensure that their organisations and communities are high-performing.'

Paul Axup, CFO, Aurecon

'Karen's book is easy to read, data-rich, and informative. It provides practical and clear suggestions for achieving change on diversity and inclusion in groups and organisations. It is a valuable reference tool for those of us – whether we are leaders, members of groups, or parents – who want to see continuing change in this area in our society and our organisations. Most of all, it helps us learn more about ourselves and be better people and leaders for it.'

Andrea Durrant, Managing Partner, Boards Global

'I had the pleasure of being supported by Karen on my leadership journey for the last 12 months. During this period we had lots of meaningful conversations around purpose-driven leadership and what makes a strong team. Having worked in many different countries around the globe, there is one big learning for me: don't believe thinking or doing things your way is the only or best way! Diversity is one of the key enablers to a high-performance team. The more different backgrounds, experiences and worldviews the people in your company have, the better they will find solutions and drive performance.

'Gender bias is still one of the most pertinent biases, and as the father of a daughter, I am much more sensitive to this dimension of biases since she was born. The topic of bias is much wider than that – any bias prevents you from exploring the opportunities around you and it can be very hurtful to another person; it is never factual. We are all used to seeing the world through our own eyes, but I encourage every leader to change perspective and to experience the wealth of a more diverse view – it is truly enriching and one of the greatest experiences I have as a leader every day.'

Rafael Pasquet, CFO, Mercedes-Benz Financial Services Australia Pty. Ltd.

'A thought-provoking and practical book on gender bias for any leader in today's workplace. I really enjoyed Karen's book because it provides effective leadership tools to help identify and overcome gender bias, reframe the conversation, and create more inclusive workplaces.'

Angela Williams, General Manager Community & Housing, Broadspectrum

Karen Morley

Beat gender bias

First published in 2020 by Major Street Publishing Pty Ltd
E: info@majorstreet.com.au
W: majorstreet.com.au
M: +61 421 707 983

NATIONAL
LIBRARY
OF AUSTRALIA

A catalogue record for this
book is available from the
National Library of Australia

ISBN: 978-0-6485159-9-9

Cover design by Simone Geary and Production Works
Internal design by Production Works
Printed in Australia by Ovato, an Accredited ISO AS/NZS 14001:2004 Environmental Management System Printer.

10 9 8 7 6 5 4 3 2 1

There's no greater gift than thinking that you had some impact on the world, for the better.

— GLORIA STEINEM

Foreword

As we head into the 2020s, there has never been a more important time to turn our attention to ensuring our organisations are inclusive.

As survey after survey shows, leaders of organisations feel that there has never been greater uncertainty. There have been major shifts in globalisation, technology, geopolitics, demographics and industries. In a world where change is inevitable, organisations must be able to adapt and innovate. For organisations, that means drawing on all the diverse talent that is available and creating an environment where everyone can fully participate and contribute.

As Karen Morley says, 'The compelling logic for increased diversity is because it increases performance.' It is perhaps no surprise that increased diversity improves performance. As the legendary investor Warren Buffett has said, 'We've seen what can be accomplished when we use 50 per cent of our human capacity. If you visualise what 100 per cent can do, you'll join me as an unbridled optimist...' Furthermore, research by a range of leading advisory firms and academic institutions indicates that companies' performance is enhanced by being more diverse. That research shows that having a diverse workforce provides tangible and measurable benefits. Companies are more profitable, more collaborative and more inclusive when they hire women.

And in terms of organisations we can relate to, companies that we know well are talking about the difference that diversity makes. For example, our largest miner, BHP, has committed to a 50:50 gender split at all levels of the organisation by 2025. Why have they made this commitment? For better performance. The company has seen improvements in its safety record, produced higher operational results and returned better scores on employee engagement where it has greater diversity.

For many of us, our lived experience also demonstrates that gender balance makes a positive difference. I speak regularly to both men and women who talk about the improved team dynamics when there is gender balance – whether that means an organisation needs to look at increasing the number of women or the number of men. And I speak from experience with both.

Finally, there is also the persuasive ethical argument that we should all have the opportunity to reach our full potential and make the greatest contribution we can.

So, given that there are compelling reasons for organisations to pursue greater diversity and ensure inclusivity, why has progress been slow? The answer is that it's tough to bring about the sort of change that is required – and in particular, to overcome the biases that we all have, and which are so often embedded in organisational cultures.

Karen Morley has done us all a great service by writing this book. She has the deep knowledge and experience to translate what we know about building more inclusive organisations into how to do it. And she does it in such a straightforward and practical way. In particular, I appreciate that Karen tells stories and gives tips that provide a way forward for leaders and organisations that might feel stuck, despite their best intentions. Her 'bias busters' provide a great checklist for what can and needs to be done.

I am sure all readers will appreciate Karen's candour – whether she is talking about her own biases, saying when it doesn't make sense to push for greater diversity, or suggesting that we don't try to convert Resistors. This is a really practical guide, but it draws on a deep understanding of psychology and group behaviour, as well as the research on gender equity.

I've known Karen for many years – and she has never failed to offer insight and practical guidance. With this book, I am confident that all readers will deepen their knowledge and find ways to become more effective leaders. And it is through personal leadership that we can all make a difference – to build stronger organisations and a better society.

Kathryn Fagg, AO
Chairman Boral Ltd, Past President Chief Executive Women,
Non-Executive Director Male Champions of Change

About the author

Karen's vision is to amplify leadership impact. A critical way to do that is to make sure that everyone's talents are developed to the full. That's why inclusive leadership strategies and practices are core to her work. She is an authority on the benefits of gender-balanced leadership and how to help women to succeed at work.

What really lights Karen up is the idea of helping to make the working world a better place: one where everyone's talent and potential shine, one where everyone has a chance to rise up and be their best.

It's her own experience of difference that drives Karen's motivation to beat bias. She's experienced the pain of being excluded; it feels like being stuck in first gear. The engine keeps revving, but all it does is create more friction. She's learned how to shift gears, relieve the pressure and accelerate change. She helps inclusionists to be more influential so that they create bigger change more rapidly. And she works with leaders who want to be more inclusive, showing them how to see what's invisible and what to do to overcome bias.

Karen has helped organisations like Bunnings, CSL, Department of Education, Department of Justice, Downer, Fulton Hogan Australia, HASSELL, Melbourne Water, QBE, Officeworks and The University of Melbourne on their diversity and inclusion programs.

She has previously published *Gender Balanced Leadership: An Executive Guide* to help organisations be fairer *and* get great results and *Lead Like a Coach: How to Get the Most Out of Any Team* to help leaders increase engagement and get better work done.

Working with Karen Morley

Karen works with executives and human resources leaders from a range of different organisations to help their leaders create fairer and more innovative workplaces. She consults with organisations on strategies to increase gender inclusion, reduce unconscious bias and promote inclusive leadership. Her Inclusionist Quest program is for inclusion influencers who want to step up the rate of progress, stop backlash and create workplaces where everyone thrives.

To find out more about how Karen can work with you or your organisation, please visit www.karenmorley.com.au or call +614 38 215 391.

Contents

Introduction

I was six when I first experienced bias. Rather than my gender, which is what I will be focusing on in this book, it was my left-handedness. Try as I might, I could never score more than 6 out of 10 on my writing tests. There was no encouragement from my teacher, only criticism. The three other left-handers in the class received the same treatment. It wasn't about the quality of our writing – even at six I could tell that! It was always about the inferiority of being left-handed.

I kept trying to 'get it right', frustrated that I couldn't gain approval and succeed. I couldn't crack the secret code; to my teacher, I was a left-hander first and Karen Morley second. The feeling of not being seen for my skills and efforts was very strong, even at such a young age.

I care so much about bias because at such an early age in my life I had constraints placed on me simply because I was different.

Luckily for me, I did well in other subjects and I had a very supportive family.

The next year, I was in a new class with a new teacher and everything was different. The world opened up fully to me. I did well at school and later at university. I completed a master's degree in psychology with an exceptional group of mental health professionals, working with women and children experiencing domestic violence.

My first working role was in a community health service led by a female CEO, with a gender-balanced workforce. It was a great privilege to work in such a purpose-driven, fair and growth-oriented culture. The experience shaped my view of what work should be like.

Several years later, when I sought to advance my career in another organisation, I once again found myself constrained by bias. This time, it was because of my gender. I felt passed over for promotional roles, with vague feedback as to why. My situation changed dramatically when a new CEO joined the organisation and appointed a female boss to my division. Over the next six years I enjoyed rapid career advancement.

Since then, I've been committed to doing what I can to advance the careers of women and promote inclusion. I want to change the way we shape and experience the world of work. Work should be a place where talent and potential shine, where people are noticed and recognised because of what they can do, not what they look like. My dream is that no-one should be held back due to their skin colour, gender, sexuality, handedness or any other feature. We should all have the opportunity to rise to be our best!

While this book focuses on beating gender bias, its broader purpose is to give you the knowledge and tools to beat all kinds of bias. My goal is to drive a stronger awareness of the value of inclusive leadership to amplify everyone's full talents and potential.

- **Part I** explores what to know, what to value and what to do in order to beat bias.

- **Part II** is a deep dive into the most vexing biases; it provides suggestions on how to mitigate them.

- **Part III** focuses on how leaders can create a gender-balanced, inclusive culture at an organisational level.

- **Part IV** provides a roadmap for how to change everyday conversations, explaining how to notice bias, how to let others know about it and how to stop it happening.

Each chapter closes with a 'Bias Buster' section, detailing specific actions you can take to outsmart bias. Take them one at a time! Choose the action that best fits you and your role, the one that will most benefit your team or organisation.

Let's progress gender balance and create more inclusive cultures!

Good luck!

PART I

What does it take to beat bias?

We must carry forward the work of the women who came before us and ensure our daughters have no limits on their dreams, no obstacle to their achievements, and no remaining ceilings to shatter.

— BARACK OBAMA

To beat gender bias, three key areas need attention: what to do, what to know and what to value, as shown in the diagram following. This is the focus of this first part of the book.

What it takes to beat bias

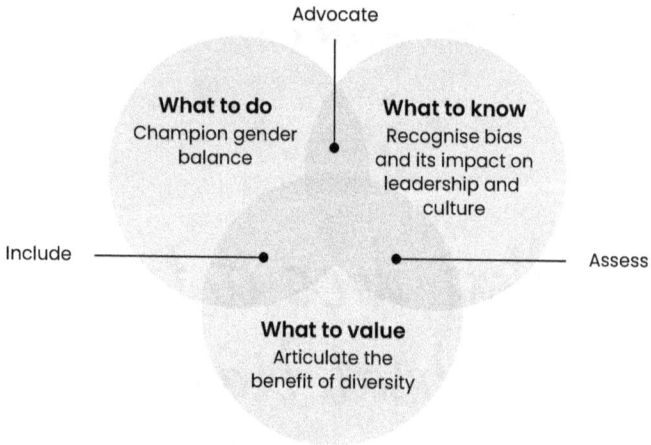

Advocate

What to do
Champion gender balance

What to know
Recognise bias and its impact on leadership and culture

Include

Assess

What to value
Articulate the benefit of diversity

To beat bias, you need to actively champion gender inclusion. When you advocate for inclusion you make bias and its impact transparent.

We're still learning how bias works, and how it affects decisions. It's critical to know what bias is and how it impacts beliefs about leadership because if we can't see it, we can't change it. When we know what it is, we can analyse how it impacts leadership and organisational cultures.

We need to continue to assess and learn about the impact of bias to clarify the value we gain when we beat it. If we don't assess its impact, we won't choose the right course of action. The clearer the benefit of diversity to your team or your organisation, the better. When we remove bias, what's the payback to the bottom line?

When the value of removing bias value is clear, you can champion specific actions that include rather than exclude.

In this first part of the book:

1. **Chapter 1** describes how to be a Champion of gender inclusion and how to support those who are. Why not do both?

2. **Chapters 2, 3 and 4** cover what to know. You might not feel ready to champion gender inclusion because you don't know enough about it. Start here, to increase your understanding. Chapter 2 details how to understand bias, and how to recognise and prevent biased behaviour. Chapter 3 exposes the dark side of organisational cultures that are not balanced. It highlights the toxicity that extreme contest cultures create. Chapter 4 presents the antidote to such cultures, outlining a prescription for gender-balanced culture.

3. **Chapter 5** explores how to articulate the benefits of gender-inclusive workplaces.

1

What to do: be a Champion, not a Bystander

It's about the legacy you leave and diversity is a key part of that... If I leave with the right diversity in place, then it's a job well done.

— ALAN JOYCE, CEO, QANTAS

When all is done and dusted, what will you be known for? My past experiences of difference began my journey to beat bias. They drive my present aspiration to increase inclusion. A common motivator of Champions of diversity and inclusion is their own experience of difference.

I ask leaders in my Inclusive Leadership workshops to reflect on when they first experienced difference. I ask participants to identify what it felt like. The number of negative experiences far outweighs the positive.

A recent workshop identified these negative feelings:

- stressed
- isolated
- excluded
- lonely
- vulnerable
- uncomfortable
- inferior
- awkward
- embarrassed
- angry.

Positive feelings that were identified included 'awesome', 'refreshing', 'proud', 'special' and 'fascinated'.

It's uncomfortable to recall negative emotions: we tend to shy away from doing so. The purpose of this activity is to ground the senior leaders with whom I work in the real impact of exclusion. Those few who have never personally experienced the negativity of difference get to hear what it's like from their peers. It makes the disadvantage that others face more salient and meaningful. It reminds us of our 'ordinary privilege', which motivates action.

We then focus on what it's like to feel included, to highlight the difference between these two emotional states and experiences. This helps to clarify the gap that inclusive leadership can breach. When senior leaders are motivated to champion the benefits of inclusion, they create a powerful legacy.

Nick Marinelli: a Champion in action

In 2019, Nick Marinelli stepped down from his role as CEO of Fulton Hogan Australia (FHA), a billion-dollar infrastructure and construction company. Reflecting on his diversity legacy, he told me that there were two clear experiences of difference that motivated him to be a Champion. They were key to his decision to ensure a positive diversity legacy for his organisation and sustained his resolve over many years.

After leaving school, Nick was a builder's labourer for several years. Building sites were very much a 'man's world' at the time. He became aware of a sense of inferiority as he compared his treatment to that of 'educated' others working around him. He also noticed that women were not treated in the same way as men, and had fewer opportunities.

His personal sense of inferiority spurred him to further his education. He completed a degree. Of this transition, he says that he identified that there was something different he could do with his life and his career. He is very grateful for the support of his organisation, and he worked hard for it in return. He recalls how good it felt; it was highly motivating to him to experience the success of working hard and achieving well.

Nick loves it when people succeed and when leaders feel pride in the achievements of their people. One of his joys in being CEO was seeing leaders light up when their people felt recognised for their achievements.

The second experience that motivated Nick occurred more recently within FHA. Female engineering graduates are in short supply. They represent about 15 per cent of all engineering graduates in Australia. FHA was recruiting female graduates at above those odds but was finding it hard to keep them at quite the same rate.

To increase support for them, a two-day workshop was arranged. Nick joined the group and 'noticed a problem' almost immediately. Some of the women identified a clear lack of support from their managers to attend the workshop.

Nick couldn't believe it. As he related this story to me, he became more animated. Even now, years later, he remains incredulous at the lack of support provided to these talented women. He's convinced that if they had been men there would have been no question about their attendance. 'For two days?' he said, 'You've got to be kidding.'

He became aware of a second issue. It will be all too familiar to women who have worked in non-office-based male-dominated workplaces. Required safety wear was not available in appropriate sizing.

Nick tells the story of one participant who was the sole woman on a particular worksite. She was dismayed when she first saw the safety wear. She had to roll up the sleeves and legs of the clothing to wear it. She described herself as looking like the Michelin Man. There was no way she wasn't going to stand out, and it was no way to try to fit in. She felt discouraged, yet she persisted. Nick describes that workshop conversation as one of his light-bulb moments.

In Nick's business he wanted everyone to have the same opportunity and he could see this wasn't happening.

As CEO, he knew that it was important to find out more about what was getting in the way. While he wanted everyone to have opportunity, he was realistic enough to know that not everyone shared his motivation. He didn't feel that managers were deliberately blocking the women. Yet he knew he had to involve himself directly so he could figure out what needed to change. This is advice that he would give to other diversity Champions: get in on the ground to see what people experience before you tick the box to say it's done.

To make it work, and make it stick, Nick believes that diversity needs to make sense as part of the overall business strategy. His leaders and he worked hard to get buy-in to their business strategy. Then they worked on the diversity and inclusion strategy to support it. This minimised resistance.

Nick says, 'People have to be able to say *why* we're doing this. If it's a part of the strategy, it makes sense to them.' Then it's much easier to figure out what you need to do to make it work.

When Nick's organisation had earlier focused on gender diversity, they did it as a stand-alone. It sat outside of the strategic framing, and there was a lot more resistance. There was resistance in particular about 'getting the best person for the job'. (The irony of this is not lost on Nick!) Second time around, they broadened out their focus to inclusion and they added Indigenous, age, ethnicity and disability program goals. This shifted the resistance.

Nick's advice to other CEOs is to be clear about where inclusion connects with strategy. Trying to carry out any initiative in isolation of the strategy is unlikely to work.

One indicator of success that Nick likes to share is the shift in the representation of women at FHA's annual awards. The awards have nine categories, one of which is Rising Star. Five years ago there were no women regional finalists. At the 2019 ceremony, about one third of the nominees were women. Women were all but one of the regional Rising Star winners. This is tangible evidence of achievements to date.

Nick sees the key lessons for championing diversity as follows:

- ► Start early, and get into the detail, talk to people.
- ► Keep it in focus, don't let your attention wane.

► Embed it in the strategy so that it gets into the organisation's DNA, and outlasts you.

Nick used his desire to leave a positive legacy to propel his commitment to inclusion. As he leaves FHA, he can point to indicators that change is in the company's DNA. Yes, there's more work to do. The construction industry has systemic challenges that make gender inclusion especially hard work. He achieved change using his motivation to create equal opportunity for career advancement: to take personal accountability for it. He wanted to make it bigger than himself so that it's in the organisation's DNA and will stick.

It's Nick's legacy that is his motivation, combined with a strong commitment to inclusion. Instead of waiting for a better time, being distracted by myriad issues or making it about him, Nick focused on making it part of FHA's DNA (see Figure 1.1).

Figure 1.1: A Champion's legacy is to embed diversity in the organisation's DNA

What it takes to be a Champion

What does a Champion look like? Do Champions have to be CEOs, like Nick? Can men be Champions for gender balance? There are some who think that it's a bit ironic for men to be Champions. But is it?

For the last 40 years we've been focused on 'fixing women', creating more opportunity for them. Women have been doing the heavy lifting, championing feminism and equal opportunity advances. It's not enough. For a start, we haven't devoted the same effort to opening up opportunity for men. What would fewer gender-based prescriptions mean for men? What difference could it make to men who pursue female-dominated roles and careers? And what difference would it make if those roles were gender-balanced?

Not enough time has been spent on balancing the best of the genders. Men and women should have freedom of choice about the kinds of people they want to be and the kinds of roles they want to play.

Unfortunately, that's a bigger agenda than the one I have for this book. For now, my focus is on the bias that prevents women from having equal opportunity to succeed in non-traditional work roles and careers. It's here that men retain the dominant position in organisational and business leadership life. That won't change without dedicated attention.

Back to the question: should Champions be male or female? Personally, I think this question is a distraction.

Anyone who wants to champion gender diversity should feel welcome to do so.

Is it more *effective* for men or women to champion gender equality? While female Champions have led the way to gender-balanced leadership, it isn't an either/or question.

Professor Isabel Metz of Melbourne Business School believes that male CEOs who are committed to equality may be particularly effective change agents. That's 'because of the perceived absence of self-interest and credibility in doing so'.[1]

Female CEOs and leaders may be seen to advance their own interests when they pursue equality for women. (We can certainly question that position but will let it go for now!) Males are unlikely to be seen in the same way. There's a popular argument that men 'lose' and women 'gain' when the gender balance of top roles changes.[2] If men are more vocal and active in support of gender balance they become a credible voice in favour of gender equality for other men. In some contexts that may reduce the perceived threat and increase momentum for change.

It is not only male CEOs who have persuasive power. Men who want to be part of a more equal world should feel confident that they *can* contribute. They should add their voices and use their persuasive powers to champion gender equality. Women should continue to champion the cause.

Many voices strengthen the call for change. Gender-balanced persuasion, using the voices of both men and women, is an apt way to achieve gender-balanced leadership.

As men are the dominant power holders, their role in change is fundamental.

+ The Male Champions of Change movement

Male Champions of Change (MCC) is a national movement helping to share the responsibility for championing gender balance.[3] This represents a fundamental and welcome progression in promoting inclusive leadership. The movement is significant. It signals the readiness of senior men to challenge themselves and to lead the way towards better gender balance and inclusion.[4]

By bringing men together to focus on gender equality, men are influencing each other in powerful ways. They are exposed to positive messages and an array of constructive possible actions.

Male Champions and Supporters change minds. They may also change more intransigent implicit attitudes about women and senior leadership. Their credibility and power change the minds of their more sceptical peers and this is good news.

Professor Metz interviewed more than 40 Australian MCC members to understand their motivations.[5]

She found that Champions are motivated by existing positive attitudes, they get the value of gender balance and stand up to advocate for it.

Supporters get it too, but they're going about what they do quietly and without much recognition. MCC Supporters were motivated by personal reasons such as existing positive attitudes: 'I want to make a difference.' Their work has great value and would benefit from amplification, letting people know what they're doing and why they're doing it.

Bystanders were neither for nor against gender balance; they'll do what they're told to do and change when the environment around them requires it. MCC Bystanders were motivated by external pressures from stakeholders: 'It seems like it's the right thing to do.' Pressure from others and feeling out of step with peers are what motivates them to change their behaviour.

Metz identified that many Bystanders became more passionate about gender equity once they were members of an MCC group. She attributes this to their having gained a better understanding of the issues.

Sceptics ask why, which projects opposition. It directs everyone's efforts to convincing them otherwise. Sceptics in the MCC groups were prompted by 'ulterior personal motives'. They joined to gain status and visibility: 'I'll do this to make myself look better to people I want to impress.' Sceptics can be guided by their need for status.

And Resistors just say no; they actively oppose moves towards gender balance.

What makes male Champions effective?

Male Champions influence each other in powerful ways. Together with Supporters, they change attitudes. They are effective at changing the attitudes of Bystanders. They have credibility and trustworthiness. They give clear and consistent messages that have personal congruence.

The MCC groups may be one of the strongest ways for male leaders to influence their peers, particularly those who don't believe in equality or those who think there is a lack of suitably qualified women.

Senior organisational leaders are powerful and credible, and their influence goes well beyond the MCC and peer groups. It is well known that powerful influencers change our explicit attitudes.[6] Their messages carry great weight and they set the tone. People see them as experts and place their trust in them. Who could be more persuasive about leadership than a CEO?[7]

Persuasion is effective at changing explicitly held attitudes.

We should, however, be extremely cautious about Resistors; attempts to persuade them can backfire. Weak messages may create, or reinforce, attitudes that oppose equality. Unconscious attitudes may also be further strengthened.[8] Resistance may be further entrenched.

Conscious attitudes adapt to a wide range of change techniques. Until recently, proven methods to change unconscious associations have been limited. There are two main methods: overtraining associations in their opposite direction, or interrupting associations.

Our minds work on two tracks, one conscious, slow and explicit, and the other unconscious, fast and implicit. It would be particularly helpful to understand if persuasion affects our unconscious attitudes. Because they are unconscious, they are harder to identify. Researchers have recently turned their attention to this question.[9]

How does persuasion change implicit attitudes? There is no short answer because implicit opinion is complicated, as we'll discover in Chapter 2. Implicit evaluations do change when we have plenty of 'cognitive bandwidth' available, when we are not overloaded and we have the time to think deliberately. No matter how persuasive the message, it takes a lot of thinking effort to override implicit attitudes. Credible sources, like CEOs and other senior leaders, are more likely to change our implicit attitudes, as we are more likely to give them our full attention.

Under the right conditions, persuasion can change implicit attitudes.

How you can be a Champion

Nick's story highlights the mindset for being a Champion. True, he was CEO of his organisation and that gave him status and power to lead change.

Whether or not you are a CEO, you can create a meaningful legacy by paying attention to your actions now, and how they will have an impact in the future. Figure 1.2 captures this dynamic between our actions now and their future impact.

Figure 1.2: How to be a Champion

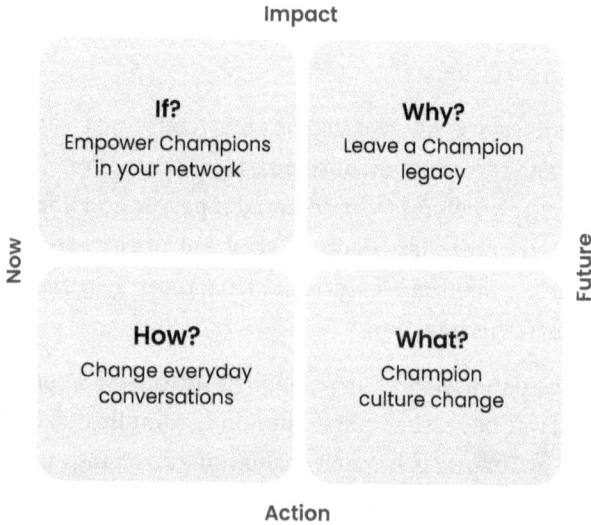

Impact

If? Empower Champions in your network	Why? Leave a Champion legacy
How? Change everyday conversations	What? Champion culture change

Now   Future

Action

To leave a Champion legacy you need to advocate for the value of diversity and inclusion. Get a firm focus on the future impact you want to have and align yourself to that.

Champions focus on creating a gender-balanced culture, a climate of inclusion. That's the best way to beat bias. Championing culture change is what you need to do to contribute to a more inclusive future. If you're the CEO, you have formal levers that you can use to understand and adapt your organisation's culture. If not, work with others to influence your culture.

Now if this sounds a bit challenging, don't worry. There are simple ways to change the conversation, and you can create a bigger change than you might think. Making very small adjustments to how you engage in everyday conversations is a powerful way to create change. Changing the conversation will pay back if we are able to unlock the potential of so many more people at work. What a difference it would make if everyone was enabled to reach their fullest potential and do their best work!

Whether or not you are a senior leader in your organisation, one of the strategic things you can do is become a Champion for gender inclusion. And then you can support and empower other Champions in your network. Let's make it a quest. Set your sights on your legacy and let's make a better world together.

How to create more Champions

Many of us don't believe we can be powerful enough to make this kind of change. It seems to take a lot of effort and is something that other, more powerful people do. If you feel like you need to know more about bias, and to better understand the benefits of gender inclusion before you work on creating Champions, read Chapters 2 through 5 first, then return here.

If you are ready now to help create and support Champions, start by reviewing the people in your network. The aim is to identify a small number you can help shift towards Champion status.[10]

I've created a Champion Continuum (Figure 1.3) to represent what it takes in practice to create Champions. It's a guide to help you understand how to engage others in change. Plot where leaders in your network are on the continuum. Below, I suggest ways to encourage them to move to the right of the continuum.

Figure 1.3: Champion Continuum

Resistor Sceptic Bystander Supporter Champion

Champions might be CEOs or other leaders, they might be men or women. Think of this continuum as another pipeline. We focus so much on the pipeline of women who are ready for more senior roles. Add this pipeline of male support into your mix.

How can you amplify support for gender balance by creating your own Champions pipeline?

This is an instance in which you can use affinity bias to advantage. When men in leadership roles are Champions and Supporters, they influence other men like them. Affinity bias can be made to work for change rather than against it.

Tactics for Champions include thanking and encouraging them, and offering to help. Share their stories with others.

Amplify the work of Supporters in your network by letting people know what they're doing and why they're doing it. Ask yourself: 'Who are the Supporters I know?'

A senior leader I was mentoring on inclusive leadership shared his philosophy of inclusion with me. He believed his teams were particularly innovative because of their diversity. He was saying all the right things to me and there was a great deal of passion in his stories.

I asked him who knew about his approach and his stories. I was aware that being a Champion wasn't his reputation. I asked him two questions: 'What if you had a reputation for being a Champion?' and 'What would you like your legacy to be?' For him, this opportunity to shift his reputation to be more positive was motivating. If he shared his stories he could move from being a Supporter to being a Champion in his organisation.

Bystanders are the 'walking on eggshells' group. They hold themselves back because they are too concerned about getting it right; they worry too much about offending others. They would take action if they had guidance but without it they are not sure what to do. Suggest that they take specific and clear actions, and expect them to be done. Bystanders tend to respond well to being held accountable for change.

As for the Sceptics, don't take their scepticism at face value and don't try to convince them with alternative facts. Seek to understand where they are coming from and what their concerns are.

Finally, to Resistors: in my view they are best left alone. There's plenty of work to do with people in the other categories. The challenge with Resistors is that putting pressure on them to change can in fact increase their expression of bias. Change the context around them, grow support; this will make change possible.

Sometimes a focus on an external cause can help to make better sense of why diversity and inclusion are important. Everyone wants to make a difference. Everyone needs a sense of purpose. If you believe that someone in your network could make a difference, find out what motivates and engages them in their broader world. Find their hook.

For diversity, sometimes it's a motivation to ensure a successful future for their daughter. For others, it might be to enable girls living in poverty to have an education, or to promote understanding of the impact of women's involvement in peace negotiations. It might be their desire to decrease family violence.

Having discovered the motivating factor, help them connect with an inclusion purpose through the channel of these broader interests.

Find key people in your network, and work on increasing their support for gender inclusion. Start with one person.

You don't have to influence everyone. Identify people with whom you already have a connection and work the power of connection to speed up change. Who do you have the opportunity to influence, even if in small ways? Where are they on the continuum? Seek to inspire them to increase their support for gender balance.

Bias Buster 1a

Create your Champion legacy

- What do you want your legacy to be? Write your legacy purpose statement:

  'I [*do something*] to [*advance inclusion*] so that [*the world is a better place*].'

  I _____

  _____

  to _____

  _____

  so that _____

  _____

- What will it take to achieve your legacy?
- What do you need to do next to start living your legacy?

Bias Buster 1b

Support Champions in your network

- Who is in your Champions pipeline?
- Where are they on the continuum?
- What is one thing you can do with each of them to move them one step closer to the Champion end of the continuum?

2

What to know: how to make bias visible so you can beat it

We like to think that our mind is like an impartial judge in search of the truth, but it is more like an attorney searching for evidence to support her case.

— ANTHONY GREENWALD[1]

We need Champions because it has not been easy to create gender-balanced organisations. That's because unconscious bias is endemic and insidious. Insight into what bias is and how it works opens up so much opportunity for positive change.

One of the breakthroughs of the last decade has been a better understanding of the impact of unconscious bias on decision-making.[2] Unconscious thought processes play a powerful role in our practical decision-making. There are more than 200 cognitive biases that distort decisions.[3] When there is too much information, not enough meaning, too little time or not enough capacity, we take mental shortcuts. We are not as rational and systematic as we'd like to think.

Our cognitive biases affect our people decisions. People decisions are more strongly influenced by unconscious cognitive biases than other decisions.[4] That's because bias erodes decision quality, transparency and fairness. It results in decreased engagement, talent losses and reduced productivity.[5]

To be able to counteract the impact of these invisible influences, we need to know more about how they work. Only then can we take actions and design processes that mitigate their impact.

This chapter explores bias at a systemic level to clarify what it is. It also explores in more detail how the associations we hold translate into particular biases at work. It provides tactics for either removing or avoiding them.

What bias is

As mentioned above, our brains work on two levels, which psychologist Daniel Kahneman labels 'fast' and 'slow'.[6] While we believe that we know what we are thinking, we often don't. Most of our 'mental work' occurs in the fast lane. Intuitions, impressions and judgements are made without awareness; they underpin the majority of our decision-making.

Our brains have evolved into super-processors. This is because fast thinking relies on heuristics, which are mental shortcuts that make decision-making much simpler. The shortcuts use automatic associations that we learn without being aware of it.[7]

Our conscious minds process about 40 pieces of information each second: a small share of the total information available to us. This is the thinking and judging we know we do. It is more deliberate and effortful than fast thinking.

While our conscious mind deals with its 40 bits of information, it's estimated that our unconscious mind deals with between 8 and 40 *million* bits.[8] Our unconscious mind efficiently processes these bits in the background without us knowing it's happening. We don't have to go into the same situation multiple times and experience it as brand new each time. This saves valuable conscious resources.

Intuitions can appear magical, because we are not aware of the process by which they are made. Good intuitions come to mind when we recognise what is happening, analyse it correctly and act appropriately. For example, we are able to recognise that a caller at the other end of the phone is angry when they say their first word. We marvel at an accomplished pianist who plays with great skill a piece of music they've never seen before.[9]

Intuitions can also be terribly wrong. Thankfully they are wrong less frequently than they are right. Still, at times, we apply the wrong criteria, without knowing it. For example, we might make a choice to buy a house based on our emotional response to the house, rather than on general trends in house prices in the area. Our feelings underlie many more of our decisions than we realise.

Somewhat tongue in cheek, I rather like to use the metaphor of the brain working like hierarchy works in an organisation.

The executives on the 35th floor are busy being strategic and making decisions. They believe they are pulling the big levers. That's the slow lane. Yet it's the workers on the lower floors who are getting the work done. That's the fast lane. Much of what gets done isn't controlled, nor even known about by the executives, despite their focus on decision-making.

Unconscious heuristics affect leadership decision-making. On the upside, unconscious or implicit processes enable us to make very quick, automatic judgements. That frees us to better attend to other tasks; our limited conscious memory capacity can be used in other ways. On the downside, biases like confirmation bias lead managers to ignore evidence that doesn't fit their views and to focus on what confirms it. Biases occur when we use information in the wrong way or use the wrong information, then make sub-optimal business decisions.[10]

A bias is an interpretive judgement.[11] It is an umbrella term used to describe decisions based on demographic heuristics, such as being a woman.

When it comes to people, working with conscious thought processes might seem challenging enough! Working with the intangible unconscious and its distortions only increases the challenge. Individuals often have conscious and unconscious beliefs that are contradictory, which is perplexing.

What we know about unconscious bias and how it works is relatively new. Valuable insights that can inform practice are emerging, yet they are by no means definitive. At times it feels like Alice 'stepping through the looking glass' into a distorted world, where nothing is as it seems.

How gender stereotypes create bias

Gender is a fundamental part of our conscious and unconscious associations and attitudes. We learn about gender early in our lives, and it is a primary guide for negotiating our actions in the world. It is a fundamental concept in the development of our sense of identity.[12] As our gender schema is learnt early and well, it becomes unconscious to the point where, if we reflect on it at all, it seems the natural order of things.

Our gender schema ascribes and prescribes certain traits as male and others as female. Men are typically associated with a set of traits labelled 'agentic': tough, competitive, assertive, competent, ambitious and dominant. Women are typically associated with a set of traits labelled 'communal'. These traits include empathy, understanding, gentleness, kindness, submission and sentimentality.[13] Individuals may construct different stereotypes, reflecting their own set of beliefs; yet most people recognise the accepted gender schema. This gives it a high degree of consensus and credibility.

Both male and female traits are desirable, but in different ways. We *respect* men for demonstrating the appropriate qualities, while we *like* women for their warmth and sensitivity.[14] We associate male traits with power, authority and higher status. We associate female traits with nurturing, support roles and lower status.

Organisational environments have typically operated in masculine ways. This is nowhere more evident than in the higher leadership echelons. Leadership is associated with the male traits of competitiveness, confidence, decisiveness and individualism.[15]

While there are times when our unconscious processing is highly valuable, it is when we use group characteristics to evaluate individuals that the shortcuts might create bias. Categorising people as members of groups minimises their individuality. It prevents us from gathering a host of valuable information specific to the individual; that increases the possibility of misjudgement.

We use group characteristics whether or not they apply.

The biggest challenge of all is that 75 per cent of us have an interesting duality of associations. It's not just that some decisions are being made fast and others slow. It's that the decision criteria used are different. Our fast, unconscious associations can contradict our expressed conscious beliefs. Even more challenging is the fact that both women and men can demonstrate the same unconscious bias against women in leadership. That includes those of us who openly hold egalitarian attitudes.[16]

Recent research by linguists has shown that making the association between women and top leadership remains hard to do. During the US presidential campaign in 2016, researchers completed 12 experiments with almost 25,000 participants. The results showed that a simple association between the pronoun 'she' and the role of president seldom occurred. After Hillary Clinton won the primary and most people thought she would win the election, this didn't change. Even those who expected Clinton to win did not use the pronoun 'she'. When they encountered 'she' referring to the president in text, they expressed surprise. It took them longer to process the information they were reading about.[17]

This is particularly challenging. I may make decisions I'm not aware of, that I don't even agree with.

We rely on unconscious belief patterns, fast thinking, when:

- ► We don't have clear decision criteria.

- ► We don't have or take the time to deliberate on our decisions.

- ► Information is ambiguous so it's not clear how it helps us make the decision.

- ► There is no open scrutiny of the decision.

Part of the problem is that it's not always possible to know when you've made a decision, let alone whether it was good or bad. As Figure 2.1 depicts, if we're not aware of the potential for fast thinking to impact our decisions, we are more likely to be biased. If we slow down and are cautious when we deliberate about people, we will almost certainly make better decisions, even if we don't understand bias. While the process might be a bit hit and miss, we can still make reasonably good intuitive decisions if we are aware of gender schema. We can check our intuitive decisions to make sure they are consistent with our espoused beliefs.

Slowing down deliberately to make decisions about people is the best way to debias.

Having unconscious stereotypical associations doesn't have to result in misjudgement. What matters most is how we approach decision-making about people. Important decisions such as who to recruit and promote are particularly prone to misjudgement. Deliberative decision-making processes are the antidote. When we use different perspectives and weigh costs and benefits of different actions, we reduce bias.

Figure 2.1: Impact of thinking modes on decisions

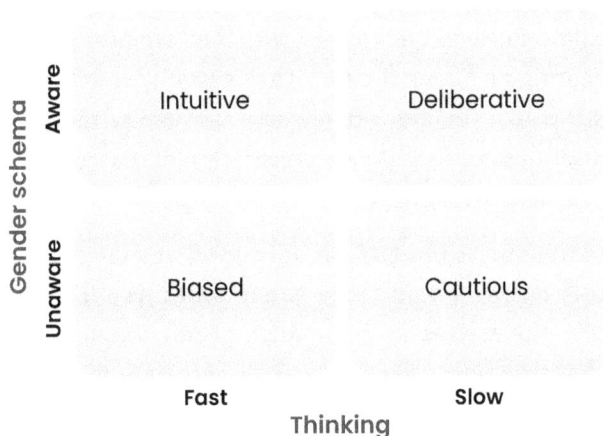

How gender bias affects leadership and organisational culture

Gender stereotypes spill over into the behavioural expectations we have of leaders and to the cultures that characterise organisations. A masculine culture promotes physical and social dominance, invulnerability and avoidance of weakness.

Key characteristics are:

- Show no weakness – don't admit you don't know, don't express doubt.

- Show strength and stamina – physical strength, endurance and bigger are better.

- Put work first – work hard, for long hours, don't let family interfere.

- 'Dog eat dog' – watch your back, you're in or out.[18]

These characteristics are quite prevalent in many industries and occupations. They are not confined to 'manly' jobs that are dangerous or involve a lot of physical strength, such as the military or emergency services. They are also present in engineering and construction. They show up in white-collar industries like finance, science and law. Many mainstream organisations conflate the demonstration of masculine traits with effective performance.[19]

A case in point is Company X; it is unashamedly masculine. There is no sense that there is any other way to be. They describe themselves as hard driving and tough. They do not offer part-time roles because it's necessary for people to always be there. Even the word *flexible* is problematic to them. They see rules and regulations as a sign of weakness; they are described by others as 'cowboys'.

A key aspect of the characteristics of a masculine work culture is invulnerability. 'Show no weakness' means that expression of emotion other than anger is not well tolerated. Men instead repress their emotion so they are not seen as 'feminine' or 'weak'. It is well known that invulnerability threatens safety. It increases unnecessary risk-taking and decreases learning. It also increases the chance of cover-ups. Escalation of errors, accidents and major problems become more likely.[20]

It's not 'male' characteristics themselves that are the problem. And it isn't men either.

A masculine work culture prizes qualities associated with 'male'.[21] The problem isn't the masculine traits themselves; any of them might have value at particular times.[22] The problem occurs when these traits represent the majority characteristics of the organisation's culture and when they are expected of everyone if they are to succeed.

An interesting feature of masculine culture is that dominance isn't ever settled. It always needs to be contested, proven time and time again.[23] Men need to keep proving themselves in the masculine areas; they are constantly jostling for dominance because the characteristics are always in play. When organisations reward those who show high levels of these qualities, they perpetuate them, as in Company X.

How masculine norms exclude women

An experienced executive with a successful track record as an Asia Pacific CEO for a global consultancy shared her story with me. She experienced quarterly global meetings as decidedly masculine, with a very strong 'bro culture'.

'It felt so much like a boys' club,' she says. 'I was one of only a couple of female executives. The hypocrisy and double standards were exhausting. It took certain skills to navigate them.

'I was diligent before all executive meetings, ensuring I was well prepared. I came to the meetings prepared to contribute fully from a strategic and innovative perspective. During these meetings I had to work hard to be heard, even when discussing my business and my region. It was an uphill battle to get the group to listen. It was difficult to be recognised for my expertise, despite my consistent results in both top and bottom line growth. The guys would pontificate, even if they didn't know anything about it. I was so discouraged by this behaviour. It was frustrating.

'Yet they didn't criticise or question each other. There was collusion between them. They had each other's backs as they went around the table talking about their business.

'It always felt awkward. I dedicated an enormous amount of energy to ensuring I fitted in and positioning my point of view in a timely way.

'It was not uncommon for the tone of the conversation to shift when I joined in. Body language and remarks suggested a lack of patience and comments were patronising. I needed to over-assert myself to secure resources and support for business imperatives.

'You take a break in the middle of the meeting and the men continue their conversation at the urinal. That's where I found they socialised their agenda and agreed to agree. It was not uncommon to arrive for the next day to learn that several of them had caught up over breakfast to discuss their strategic ideas.

'Their conversations were always about sports. At the end of the day they would attend the executive dinner, cluster around one another and then continue drinking until three in the morning. This often left them unable to function effectively during the following day as they were hung over. That didn't seem to matter for them and there were never any consequences.

'I was so astounded that they didn't seem to have to know or do anything beyond mediocracy, except be part of the club.'

An example of different contests is computer programmers and their work hours. The tech 'bro culture' has been highlighted in recent years; it is not an environment that welcomes women. At best it neglects and at worst it repels diversity.[24] Masculine characteristics become unproductive, exclusionary. Where men prove their manliness by outperforming others, a survival-of-the-fittest mindset results.

Another example of a contest culture is that among fire-fighters. In some groups, there is a high willingness to run into burning buildings. It doesn't have to be this way. Crews encouraged to express camaraderie, to show good humour and have fun, are much less likely to engage in such high-risk behaviour – both at and *outside of* work.[25] They are also faster to coordinate with each other, have fewer accidents when responding to emergency callouts and cause less property damage on the job.

Masculine norms are neither inevitable nor are they universal.[26] Not all masculine cultures are the same: some are more competitive than others. The way the contesting plays out can also vary. Moving away from a culture characterised by masculine contests improves culture and performance. It all comes down to how teams and work are structured within male-dominated occupational groups.[27]

Gender bias spills over into leadership expectations

Some evidence suggests that female leaders are more transformational in their leadership style than men.[28] Knowing that women have a more effective leadership style has not been enough to increase their promotion rate to senior levels. Their behavioural style advantage doesn't outweigh their 'lack of fit' disadvantage.[29]

One of the reasons for this is that the transformational leader-ship style is not as valued by boards and CEOs as its evidence base suggests it ought to be. The Australian Royal Commission into Misconduct in the Banking, Superannuation and Financial Services Industry shows how blindsided boards can be by competitive, dog-eat-dog cultures.[30] The organisations examined by the Royal Commission had cultures that promoted contest. In those organisations, selling the most and getting the biggest prizes were lauded. Greed fuelled short-term profit at the expense of honesty: many of the perpetrators profited while others turned a blind eye.[31] These behaviours of a masculine culture, when not moderated, lead to toxic cultures that drive poor practices.

Masculine contest cultures are hostile to men as well as women.

It's important to note, masculine cultures are not just enacted by men. There are women who lead in the same style.

➕ Gender bias spills over into how women lead

A senior female leader approached me for coaching. She was having difficulty managing her relationship with her boss. The stories she shared were concerning. She experienced unrealistic expectations and hostile interactions. Her expert advice was not acknowledged. Her boss seemed to need to control the conversation, and she felt that she was always feeding the boss's ego.

The whole leadership team got the same treatment. Nobody spoke up in leadership team meetings, which were uncomfortable. Often one person was singled out for humiliating castigation. There was little support and collegiality. Those who survived were those who didn't rock the boat, who kept their heads down, and who suffered humiliation in silence.

The boss was a woman, yet she used typical masculine leadership behaviours. After a period of time, effort and some heartache, the leader decided that her actions could not change the situation and she resigned.

Since leaving the organisation, the leader has come across other women who have experienced the same treatment. They had similar roles in organisations providing services to girls and where the majority of staff were women.

What is striking, beyond the unacceptable behaviour, is that it continues to be a surprise. We expect women to be kind and warm, and we expect the same from female leaders. When they are not, it takes longer to see their behaviour as problematic, as not about you, as beyond your ability to change. We keep expecting the warmth and kindness to emerge.

There is a double bind for female leaders, which I discuss in more detail later in the book. But there is nothing that makes this kind of behaviour acceptable, for either a man or a woman.

Back to the upside... Those women who are transformational leaders marry the best of male and female characteristics. They are both business-oriented and people-oriented. The same goes for the best male leaders: they too are business- and people-oriented. Inclusive leadership, good leadership, combines a balance of both gender-stereotypical styles.

We judge people based on stereotypes, even though people don't always behave like stereotypes.[32] While we are not stereotypes, we do rely on them as shortcuts to help make our decision-making more efficient. Most men, like most women, display a range of behaviours that transcend stereotypical boundaries. Toughness, endurance and strength as a small subset of an organisational culture are less likely to be problematic. At the extreme, when they are the driving ideals in a culture, they create masculine contest cultures.[33]

Bias buster 2

Get to grips with your own bias

- Complete the Implicit Association Test, available at implicit.harvard.edu/implicit

- Increase awareness of unconscious bias and its impact with your team and your peers. Stay curious.

- Observe and reflect on behaviours and decisions that you see day to day. How might unconscious attitudes be influencing the decisions being made?

3

What to know:
how contest cultures turn toxic

*When men are motivated to align with their
masculine identity, they are more likely to endorse
the persistence of gender inequality as a way of
affirming their status as 'real men'.*

—LAURA KRAY ET AL.[1]

In one study of leadership climate, 56 per cent of people
considered that their manager displayed toxic leadership.[2]
This is a daunting statistic and it deserves investigation.

Masculine contest cultures provide a breeding ground for
toxic leadership. They recruit, socialise and retain toxic
leaders. One of the reasons that they persist, despite being
unpleasant places to work, is that they suppress complaint.

Leaders are more abusive in masculine contest cultures.
They abuse not only their teams but also each other. In such
cultures there is more likely to be bullying and harassment.
They are less inclusive than non-contest workplaces, and

there is a lower level of organisational justice, as well as psychological safety.[3] That results in higher employee stress and work-life conflict, and more people reporting an intention to leave the organisation. Organisational commitment is low, as is wellbeing. Not surprisingly, the more toxic the culture, the more likely it is that there will be a deterioration in performance over time. Figure 3.1 shows this relationship.

Figure 3.1: Impact of masculine contest cultures on performance

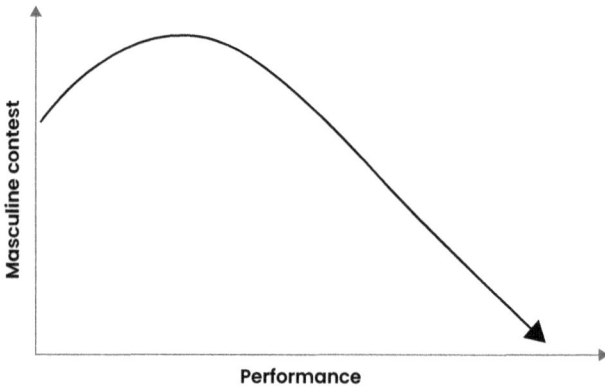

Tactics for negotiating a toxic culture

The masculine style, when not moderated, can play out very harshly. It was a significant issue for the Asia Pacific (APAC) CEO mentioned earlier. Her boss was the global CEO, located in the United States.

Her experience was that the two of them spoke a different language. At first she would seek to speak with him about certain issues and expected his support. She tended to personalise what she said to give weight to how important something was to her or to illustrate her sincerity and experience of the issue in her region. That was seen as 'emotional'. Over time, being 'personal' began to feel dangerous.

The boss was, by his own definition, a man of few words, awkward and introverted. He considered himself a 'brilliant' accountant and strategist. He was clear that he didn't have any empathy; he would tell people he didn't. He didn't see it as a shortcoming. He would say this was his style and he didn't need to change. These are general personality characteristics, yet there were gender implications for how his behaviour played out.

He was dictatorial. He would say, 'I believe this – you must agree.' He didn't tolerate interjections or disagreements. He wasn't open to feedback. It was unwise to disagree with him but if you did, he became petulant. His expectation was that his C-suite team 'toed the party line'.

The APAC CEO doubled her business in six years, tripled the bottom line and managed to build new business streams. As well, she attracted and retained senior talent. That seemed to fascinate her boss. He would ask her how she got her people to do what they did. She told him that she listened, recognised, gave people credit. While he asked, he didn't listen to her answer. When it came to the detail, he showed no concern or interest in what she did.

She describes how he proceeded to make her life exhausting. Despite her achievements, she was not recognised or rewarded in the same way as her peers. She felt that she was never quite doing enough. Anything remarkable became expected; it was her role.

Her view is that the global boss didn't work well with strong women.

There were some great women in the business. Our APAC CEO observed that there were two different approaches taken by the women to this masculine context.

For a woman to get attention around the leadership table, the preferred approach was to flirt. The CEO used to relax into the flirting, and he would pay those women attention. He crossed the line on occasion, and inappropriate relationships took place.

The reward for these women was to get increased visibility: they were given high-profile projects. It might be seen by some that it served them well, depending on their goals.

But these women didn't get next-level promotions, although they had the talent to. So while they did get a short-term increase in visibility, their behaviour held them in role. Their aspirations for the executive-team-level roles were not met.

The second approach, taken by our executive and one other woman, was to refuse to play this game. They behaved in a professional and warm manner, as 'normal individuals'.

She felt like she was forever at odds with the CEO, as though she couldn't quite get it right. She was working closely with him, but it took effort to make it work. She felt like she never had more than a 10-minute one-to-one conversation with him. He would invite interruption from someone close by to engage in small talk. She was aware that he spoke about her professional success and achievements to others, yet he was uncomfortable with her. Due to her regional location, she was left pretty much alone to 'get on with it'. Once a month she reported the region's results, which always left her feeling deflated and de-motivated.

The other female in the executive team took the same professional approach and refused to flirt. She left in disgust as she couldn't stand the environment. She was dealing with the global CEO daily and became exhausted by the interactions.

The flirting and sexualised behaviour played out around the board room. All the men tended to behave in the same way. The women likewise tended to do the same, because it seemed to get them where they wanted to be.

This toxic culture limited the leader's career options within the company. She refused to go for other CEO roles available in the organisation as they would put her in closer proximity to the boss and his behaviour. She chose not to give up the protection of regional distance.

The destructive legacy of toxic leaders

The traits exhibited by the global boss described above are recognisably narcissistic and psychopathic. Narcissistic and psychopathic leaders are the most likely to create toxic cultures.[4] While they are not always incompetent, over time they are usually destructive to the people around them. Strikingly, they are over-represented in senior management roles. Compared with 1 per cent of the general population, it is estimated that between 3 per cent and 20 per cent of leaders are narcissistic or psychopathic.

Narcissists are egotistical, self-focused and vain, qualities that are closely aligned to the features of masculine contest cultures. Organisations that glorify heroic and visionary leaders often end up with narcissists in charge. Large compensation packages and fancy titles are a giveaway.

Narcissists are 40 per cent more likely to be male.

Gender differences are highest in two aspects of narcissism. 'Exploitative entitlement' is an increased tendency to engage in behaviours that harm others. Bullying and harassment is more likely. White-collar crimes and theft are also more likely. The other aspect is leadership and authority. Narcissists are more likely to be authoritarian and despotic when they are in charge.

Adding to the problem, teams and organisations led by narcissists are statistically more likely to copy the behaviour. Unethical and harmful behaviours increase overall.

Gender differences in narcissism have reduced over the last 30 or so years; perhaps this confirms that women are expected to be like men to climb the ladder.[5] Rather than our concept of leadership adapting to be gender-balanced, women are adapting their style to be more like men. Those who have these characteristics are also more likely to be seen as leadership material.

Psychopaths have strong antisocial tendencies, like to break the rules, are more violent and aggressive, and don't feel guilt. They are also very eloquent and persuasive, are more resilient and able to channel their aggression. Courage and risk-taking often go hand in hand with psychopathy.

Psychopaths initially come across as charming and charismatic. Given that we are so enchanted by the concept of charismatic leadership, we are more likely to think that psychopaths are leader-like.

Apart from their charisma, psychopaths make bad leaders. They don't accept responsibility, don't meet deadlines, don't care about people, won't accept blame, and don't follow through. They are impulsive and unpredictable. They are more likely to harm others, the work of the team and the organisation. Phew! Because psychopaths have a profound effect on those around them, firing a toxic worker has four times the economic benefit of hiring a good worker.[6]

Psychopaths perform extremely well at interview, so beware...

Leaders low in charisma don't get noticed. That leaves the majority of airtime to leaders we should not seek to emulate. Whether leaders are behaving well or badly, employees emulate their behaviour. If leaders drive and compete, contest everything and border on the narcissistic or psychopathic, others will copy them. If they're humble and admit mistakes, share credit with others and are open to ideas, again, teams will follow.

Unfortunately, we see narcissism and psychopathy as signs of leadership potential and talent, despite the fact that they also predict the downfall of leaders who display them.

According to organisational psychologist Dr Tomas Chamorro-Premuzic, most leaders are largely ineffective. 'What it takes to *get the job* is not just different from, but also sometimes the reverse of, what it takes to *do the job*.'

Rather than there being too many obstacles to women's ascent to the top, he believes there are in fact too few for men. What we end up with, he says, 'is a pathological system that rewards men for their incompetence while punishing women for their competence.'

If organisations stopped rewarding narcissistic and psychopathic behaviours, they would promote more women. If the existing criteria remain, putting more women into leadership roles does not improve leadership. If the focus is on putting more *talented* leaders into leadership roles, then the representation of women should increase.

While masculine behaviours continue to prevail, women promoted into leadership may be just as incompetent and unsuccessful. The belief that women are not suited to be leaders, or only 'manly women' are promoted, will be reinforced.

Why beating bias is hard yet possible

In 2019, shaving company Gillette released a 1-minute, 47-second advertisement: *'We believe: the best men can be'.*[7] The ad advocated the importance of rejecting toxic masculine behaviour. It showed men intervening to stop harassment and to protect children from being bullied.

The ad caused a massive backlash response. At the time of writing, it had over 33 million YouTube views and half a million comments, many of which were pretty hateful. The campaign promoted civility, care and protection. How could that possibly generate such an uncivil, hate-filled response?

Unfortunately, some diversity initiatives backfire[8] or experience backlash.[9] *Any* attempt to change people's attitudes and beliefs will almost certainly do this. The history of Civil Rights in the United States is a good example.

What causes such backlash?

Not all bias is unconscious and not everyone is interested in being fair to those around them. Social Dominance Orientation (SDO) theory helps to understand why. The evidence behind the theory shows that people differ in two ways: how much they support dominance or hierarchy in society and how much they support equality.[10]

People who support high dominance value safety, stability, conformity, obedience and rule-following. They prefer greater levels of hierarchy and power distance in groups. They favour and feel justified oppressing others. They keep a strong focus on group competition and threat. That means support for active, and sometimes violent, opposition to the threat of reduced hierarchy. They want to maintain status differences.

Opposition to equality means maintaining support for the inequities in the current system. Inequities are seen as legitimate and fair, particularly by those who have roles at the top of the system. Their superior power and resources are considered justified and appropriate to their achievements. Opposers of equality tend to be politically conservative. They oppose policies such as equal opportunity or affirmative action. However, they do not advocate oppressive ways to maintain the system.

Men are generally higher than women in SDO.[11]

High SDO correlates with authoritarian, sexist, homophobic and racist beliefs.[12]

When people who have high levels of SDO witness acts that violate stereotypes, they feel justified in taking punitive action. Masculine superiority is to be maintained. The action includes expressing dislike or harassment. They believe it is within their rights to put women 'in their place'. Their self-esteem improves when they do. They feel better about themselves when they apply penalties for 'wrong' behaviour.

When women advocate for change they may be seen as advocating in their own interest (as discussed earlier).

Men who identify with stereotypes reduce support for equity policies if they feel any threat to their sense of superiority. Such men can see programs for gender equality as a zero-sum game. That is, they see women's gains as personal losses to them: 'You want to take what's mine.' In response, they withdraw their interest, don't get involved, or oppose the programs. Leadership needs to frame change as benefiting everyone if it is to enlist these men. Where this isn't the case, and the zero-sum game mindset is perpetuated, attempts to increase the representation of women will be difficult.[13]

An example of the zero-sum mindset occurred on International Women's Day in 2019. Australian Prime Minister Scott Morrison said:

> We want to see women rise... we don't want to see women rise only on the basis of others doing worse.[14]

Equality, he said, was:

> [N]ot about setting Australians against each other, trying to push some down to lift others up. That's not in our values... you don't push some people down to lift some people up. And that is true about gender equality too.

He went on to say that women's biggest challenges were in the developing world:

> Prosperity brings with it its opportunities, of course it does, for every person.

His remarks show a real misunderstanding of the significant economic benefit of the increase of women into workplaces.[15] Their increased representation can contribute growth, not decline.[16] Diversity has measurable benefits, as I discuss in

Chapter 5. The remarks assume that because Australia is prosperous, opportunity is equally shared.

The Prime Minister's remarks highlight one of the key arguments used to counter attempts to redress gender imbalance. Women's equality is seen by some men to reduce the status of men.

Moves towards equal pay, for example, are seen as reducing opportunities for men and placing downward pressure on men's pay. According to US politician James Green:

> If businesses are forced to pay women the same as male earnings, that means they will have to reduce the pay for the men they employ ... And as even more women thus enter the workforce, that creates more competition for jobs (and even men's jobs) and puts further downward pressure on the pay for all jobs.[17]

Women's participation in leadership is seen to reduce the status of men. In a contest culture, women's access to the competition disrupts the structural advantage men enjoy.

When men perceive threats to their masculinity they are more likely to sexually harass others – both female *and male* colleagues. Men who don't conform or are viewed as 'weak' may be isolated or ridiculed.[18] These actions are not about sex or attraction but about the need to contest for dominance and power from a masculine contest frame of reference. Women who *most* challenge gender stereotypes are so-called 'uppity women'. The research shows they are most likely to be targeted for harassment.[19]

In situations where men believe that gender roles are fixed, unchangeable or prescribed, they tend to rationalise the social system. They are more likely to justify the system and its inequities, seeing it as fair. It seems to affirm their status. That changes when men are primed to see gender roles as socially ascribed and it is then that their identification with the male stereotype decreases. They become less likely to defend gender inequities and their views align more closely with those of women.

Change can be framed as an opportunity if flexibility in roles and traits is emphasised. It doesn't need to come at a cost to status, and therefore it is less threatening.[20]

Changing gender roles are not inherently threatening. They only become so when men believe that gender roles are fixed but not when they believe they are malleable.

If men believe that their co-workers approve of a masculine workplace culture, they don't criticise it, even if they don't believe it is an 'ideal work environment'. A collective ignorance prevails.[21] Therefore, in order to fit in, the workers behave as if they do agree with the norms and they don't challenge them. This suggests that there may be less support for these kinds of cultures than it might appear.

There are unexpected negative consequences for men who 'don't rock the boat'. If they think others accept the contest culture, their own experience of satisfaction and engagement decreases. Their mental health deteriorates and they experience more relationship conflict.[22]

Another reason put forward for a lack of challenge to masculine norms is because it may be perceived as 'weak' and 'whiny' to do so. There's the fear of not being seen to 'cut it'.

For *some* men, working in a masculine culture is associated with greater work engagement and job meaning. Some men find the prospect of winning masculine status so seductive that they will sacrifice their wellbeing to be in the contest.[23] Others find it challenging; they don't want to constantly contest, compete or try to dominate others. Not measuring up against these standards means they lose out: they miss out on higher status positions.

Finally, a major challenge is that those organisations that need training the *most* are the *least* likely to benefit from it.[24] Organisations that promote masculinity don't change through traditional diversity training. In such cultures, conventional approaches have not been effective and in some cases have backfired.[25]

Men in such cultures can reject training. They see it as an infringement of their autonomy or believe that their behaviours are necessary to their work. Their motivation to learn is low. For example, overplaying the illegality of harassment may evoke strong resistance from police officers. This seems counter-intuitive; it is becoming clear that effective diversity training is not a simple matter.[26] Using training to frame behaviours as unproductive to the team, rather than as illegal, has been suggested as one way to reduce such resistance.[27]

Finally, training in sensitive issues, such as gender equality, doesn't succeed without a supportive organisational climate. When there is misalignment, when training is done to meet external reporting or is tokenistic, training is at best a waste of time.[28] Training is only effective in those organisations that support its purpose and content. If the culture doesn't support or even actively opposes it, it won't be effective.

I discuss how better to set up training in more detail in Chapter 12.

Bias Buster 3

Know how to spot a toxic contest culture

- Is aggression, abuse, bullying or harassment present in your organisation?

- Is it a characteristic of the organisation or is it confined to certain divisions or teams?

- What organisational indicators of culture exist? Options include engagement, safety and stress claims, employee turnover. If no such measures exist, advocate for their collection. They help spotlight toxicity.

- Identify organisational leaders who might have concerns about the impact on culture. Advocate to them for change.

- Support colleagues who bear the brunt of toxicity.

4

What to know: what gender-inclusive leadership looks like

There is no conflict between increasing women
in leadership and improving leadership itself.
On the contrary, it is harder to improve the quality
of our leaders without increasing the numbers
of female leaders.

— TOMAS CHAMORRO-PREMUZIC[1]

Talk about gender-balanced, open, inclusive cultures has become more prevalent, but to achieve it we need to change the masculinity of work cultures. We can't increase inclusion without also decreasing the primacy of masculinity.

Chapter 3 identified the impact of toxic masculinity on workplace culture. Making the impact of masculinity more transparent clarifies why it needs to be rebalanced. It makes it easier to realign leadership to be more effective. This chapter focuses on how to do that.

When gender styles are balanced, an inclusive culture is possible

The best leaders are not reduced to gender-specific styles of leading. Leading from the confines of gender prescriptions means being half of what's possible: that's not enough.

Combining the best of agentic and communal leadership promotes a broader range of leadership styles and capabilities. Removing gender attributions from behavioural qualities shows how culture can be inclusive, as shown in Figure 4.1. When either the male or female gender-based style is present to the exclusion of the other, there are reduced options for leading. When there's too much emphasis on communal leadership, the impact is an over-polite culture that dances around difference. When there's too much emphasis on agentic leadership, the impact is an overpowering culture: enough already said on that.

Figure 4.1: It takes balance to create an inclusive culture

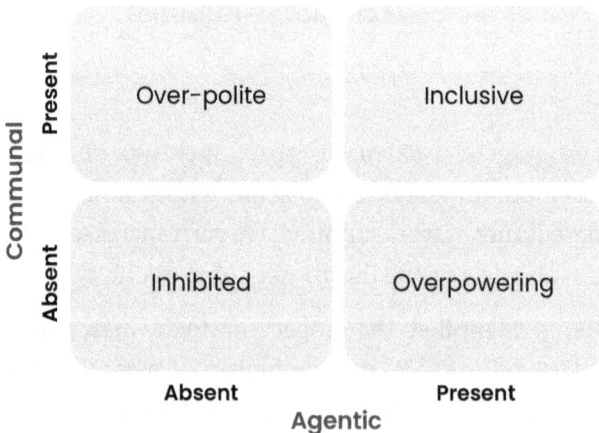

Now that we've removed the gender attributions, we can look at warmth and competence with fresh eyes. Social psychologists have researched interpersonal attributes over many decades.[2] Warmth and competence are the two key criteria by which we judge others. How they go together matters. If you overdo competence without warmth, you'll likely inspire envy. If you overdo warmth and under-do competence, you'll evoke pity. Manage neither and contempt will be the result.

Admiration is the result of warmth first, then a blend of competence and warmth. It's definitely the sweet spot for leading.

Start with warmth

Despite the primacy of the masculine style, what we know about warmth and competence is that to be more influential you need to start with warmth.[3] The masculine style isn't influential, it's coercive. Warmth comes first because:

- People need to feel a sense of belonging – until we have that we don't connect.

- If you care about others' needs and interests, you must be able to maintain your connection with them despite your status.

Leaders typically emphasise their competence or expertise with others. This is standard operating system for masculine leadership. Yet for both men and women leading through competence often backfires: it can alienate rather than influence. A wealth of leadership research showing this to be the case is too often ignored. A command-and-control style of leadership is appropriate in crisis and poor-performance situations. Otherwise its impact is negative. I've spoken about this in detail in *Lead Like a Coach*.[4]

Daniel Goleman outlined the impact of different leadership styles in his article 'Leadership that gets results'.[5] That article describes how different leadership styles impact organisational climate and performance: each is appropriate at certain times, damaging at others. Better results are obtained by thinking about leadership as a set of styles to use to adapt to different situations.

Emphasising flexibility of styles helps disrupt gender associations. We can instead focus on how to be more effective in service to the team and the organisation. How to be a good leader takes primacy, and it depends on the best of *both* warmth and competence. When both are present and expected, poor behaviour will reduce. Gender balance is more likely. This helps to avert the sense of loss that some men feel, and it promotes common ground. Figure 4.2 conveys what a balanced culture, one that is both warm and competent, can be like. It contrasts that aspiration with monocultures.

Figure 4.2: Attributes of gender-balanced culture

| Weak | Warm | Warm + Competent | Competent | Contesting |

Avoidant	Healthy	Toxic
Tender	Flexible	Tough
Timid	Compassionate	Relentless
Submissive	Responsive	Inflexible
Protective	Safe	Risky
Polite	Helpful	Hindering
Sacrifice	Abundance	Scarcity

Leadership needs to be a resource for the organisation, not for individuals

Tomas Chamorro-Premuzic contrasts the leadership styles of Travis Kalanick, former CEO of Uber, with his successor, Dara Khosrowshahi.[6] Kalanick was lauded as brilliant, creating extraordinary success at Uber. Until his toxic leadership became public knowledge, the company tolerated it. Once it became public, Uber acquired a terrible reputation, and to redeem its reputation the company fired Kalanick.

Khosrowshahi has more stereotypically feminine qualities; he is seen as agreeable and unthreatening. If more male leaders were humble like Khosrowshahi, not toxic like Kalanick, it would be much easier to recruit more women to leadership roles. In fact, it would also be easier to increase the representation of competent men. Men who do not display the same toxic contest behaviour are also disadvantaged in such a culture.

Boards and CEOs need to decide whether they want their organisations to be more effective and successful. If so, then the criteria they use for selecting leaders, male and female, needs to change.

Leadership is only successful if it is a resource for the organisation.[7]

Leadership is a resource when employees benefit from it. Then their motivation, performance and productivity will increase. When that happens, the organisation is more effective and more likely to be successful.

Masculine, commanding leadership styles downplay fundamental human needs by treating people as expendable resources, as inanimate. If organisations are to succeed, particularly in the highly disruptive decade upon us, teams of people need to perform well. Teams achieve high levels of performance when individuals are highly engaged. Individuals, in turn, are highly engaged when they feel a sense of belonging within the organisation. Organisations ignore these needs at their peril.

To experience a sense of belonging, people need to feel recognised for their uniqueness and believe that they fit in.

'When you see me for my uniqueness, I feel like I fit in.'

The sense of fit that comes with belonging is that you see me as I really am, you accept me as I am, and you see me as having value. You recognise how I contribute to the team. The connection of 'me', my unique sense of my identity, with 'we', my acceptance into the group, is what inclusive leadership strives to do.

When I belong, my engagement with the organisation increases. That drives motivation, commitment and effort. When I have a high level of engagement, I work harder in service to the organisation. I contribute my best to the team. When all team members feel this way, everyone contributes at their best and high performance can be achieved. When leaders are inclusive, their teams work better together.

And that's how organisations achieve the highest levels of success. Figure 4.3 summarises these important connections between belonging, engagement, performance and success.

**Figure 4.3: Inclusive leadership as a resource
for the organisation**

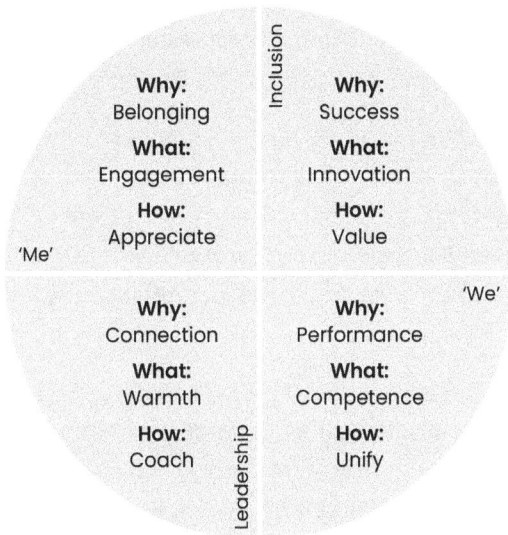

What is inclusive leadership?

Leadership should be inclusive but too often it's not. We need to reframe what we believe leadership to be in order for it to become inclusive. Inclusive leadership is the ability to engage diverse individuals across contradictory human needs. Individuals need to both stand out and be seen as unique, and fit in and connect with others to achieve performance outcomes. Inclusive leaders help people to be their best and to perform well as a team. They build trust and empower everyone, in service of the organisation's goals.

Generally, people prefer to work with similar others. This is affinity bias; it is easier to interact with people who are like us, who share demographic similarities with us, such as culture and background. It is easier and more comfortable to work with people who are most like us because it reinforces our social identity. Our social identity is fundamental to our sense of belonging and our self-esteem, which in turn is fundamental to our psychological wellbeing.

When we introduce diversity into homogeneous groups we disrupt social identity. Subgroups emerge and these create fault lines or fractures. Subgroups can interfere with sharing information. They may create tension and conflict and prevent the ability to tap into everyone's potential contribution. The leader's job becomes more complex when there is diversity in the team.

In diverse groups, appealing to what is 'common' or 'shared' is often a well-intentioned attempt to create comfort, yet it diminishes the contributions of women. If we emphasise what everyone has in common everyone should feel safer. For minority members it generally backfires: it increases the sense of not fitting in. Typical responses to this are resistance, withdrawal or assimilation, all of which diminish performance. People are unlikely to volunteer that they don't feel like they fit in; leaders need to be aware of these dynamics, watch out for them and actively help people to fit in.

Connect through warmth by coaching

In male-dominated organisations, professions and work teams, as we have seen, women feel their identities being questioned because they are different. The same identity threat is experienced by other non-dominant groups. Whether we get to see the full talents and capabilities of women in groups depends on perceptions of how safe they believe it is in the group.

Therefore, a great way to overcome identity threat, which gets in the way of anyone from a minority group, is by coaching – the leadership style that best allows personal connection. Connection is created by warmth – when we are warm towards others, it shows them we care about them, and this warmth and empathy together establish rapport between people.

The leader's role is to begin with warmth and connection, and then to create psychological safety. The safety of all team members means identity threat is reduced; it provides security. This needs to be done actively, not assumed.[8]

Identity safety is assured where women believe that their gender identity is welcome in the group.

The greater the psychological safety created in the team, the more likely people are to feel congruent. I can express the things that I cherish about myself, that I hold central to who I am, in the group. Personal congruence increases personal disclosure and contributes to team effectiveness.

Another tactic that is effective is to acknowledge the positive contribution that diverse people make. Emphasise that people's foundational identities shape their life experience and that this has direct relevance for work. A diversity perspective welcomes diversity, seeing it as a sustaining factor that leads to the surfacing of new ideas. The leader names and relies on diversity in the team to contribute to team functioning and performance. Name its value, advocate for it, and people will believe you.

Appreciate others for their unique contribution

To do their best work, people need to feel that what they do adds value. They need to be recognised for their particular contribution. Being appreciated is fundamental to feeling engaged at work. Inclusive leaders let people know that what they do matters, that they make a contribution of value, and that they are worthy of being noticed. We spend too much time at work for these needs to go unmet, and for our contribution to go unnoticed. More appreciation is needed.

The expression of appreciation, if done well and genuinely, can make a very big difference in the workplace. To be inclusive, appreciation needs to be both specific to the individual and fair across the team. If you are not sure what people value most about their work and capabilities, ask them. Make a note to provide them with regular appreciation. 'This is what I noticed you do, this is the impact it had, this is how much value it contributes to the team.' To be fair with your appreciation, notice how often you appreciate individual team members. Try to appreciate each of them the same number of times.

It's easier to notice and value those who are most like us. Because we know affinity bias works this way, it may help to have some tools to make sure you appreciate people fairly. If you have to, keep a record of when you appreciate each team member. You may need to prepare your appreciation if it doesn't come naturally. That doesn't make your appreciation disingenuous. Because you take a growth mindset and you're working to improve yourself, you know tools will help shape your new behaviour. Create a prompt, keep a scorecard of who you appreciate and how often, and that will help you to be fair. Over time your appreciation will come naturally.

Increase performance by unifying the group across its differences

Working with individuals and their uniqueness is step one. Once you are working well at the individual level, and individuals feel a sense of belonging, the next step is to work to unify across difference. Working across difference is challenging. It's needed though to achieve a high-performance team.

The team leader plays a critical role in assessing the team's tolerance for difference.

How people feel about diversity depends on how open they are to difference. Openness to difference is one of the 'Big Five' personality factors. People high in Openness enjoy difference. They promote discussion, exchange and elaboration of knowledge. They share insights and ideas relevant to the task. That enables thorough processing of diverse information, helps group problem-solving and contributes to innovation. Diverse teams that score high on Openness perform better than diverse teams low on Openness.[9]

Inclusive leaders seek to understand individuals' levels of Openness, so they can make a strategic choice. People high in Openness buck the affinity trend. They'll be excited by the differences that emerge from the diversity of the group. In that case, emphasise difference as much as possible.

Reduce the salience of diversity if team members are low in Openness, midway or you aren't sure. Diversity salience refers to how prominent diversity is. One way to reduce the salience of diversity is to create an overarching identity for the team. A second powerful way to reduce salience is to provide meaningful team rewards based on collective rather than individual effort. Rewarding a team based on team outcomes decreases the salience of intra-group differences. It empha-sises the collective identity of the team. How do we all work together to achieve our goals?

Another tactic for working with a team low in Openness is for the leader to advocate pro-diversity beliefs. This encourages team members to be more open, stimulating greater infor-mation exchange. This helps us to face our differences with a more open mind.

Finally, try cross-cutting to reduce the salience of subgroups. Cross-cutting involves identifying as many kinds of diversity in the group as possible. It makes the categorisation of people into major subgroups, including male or female, harder to do. It interferes with automatic processing. Cross-cutting also increases the chance of overlap between people. When we see others as belonging to many groups, such as cultural background, hair colour, and handedness, a major fault line is less likely. We're still working with differences here, but we are reducing their salience and the degree of threat. We can minimise what divides, and maximise what unites us.

Value diversity to increase innovation and achieve success

With connection, belonging and performance in place, success follows. The diversity dividend can be realised. Diverse people aren't just in the room, their diversity benefits the work of the team. Teams that make the most of their differences operate within a high learning frame, which means that there is active debate. The team can work constructively with difference and with the disagreement and conflict that it can generate.

How do you work with conflict, tolerate dissent, raise 'undiscussables' and survive? What does it take to achieve great outcomes? A lot of teams I've seen either won't acknowledge or raise these tough issues or they end up beaten down by them because they don't know what to do once they are raised.

If people believe that their discomfort with risky topics signals a learning opportunity, they will be more likely to tolerate it. High learning frames authorise reflection about your own point of view and curiosity about others'.

'Undiscussables', the tacit conflicts that are forbidden territory because they are 'too hot to handle', can be raised. Raising them provides the chance that they will become productive. Otherwise they become the elephant in the room and continue to get in the way; managing these discussions is a fine art.

Figure 4.4, over the page, contrasts the elements of a low learning frame with a high learning frame. Inclusive leaders manage conversational dynamics so that all voices are heard. They encourage dissent *and* great ideas.

High-value learning frames build on diversity perspectives and psychological safety. This turns the acceptance of difference into innovation and moderates the 'heat' in the group caused through diverse perspectives. An optimum zone for performance is possible.

The leader promotes the learning behaviours of advocating, inquiring, surfacing 'undiscussables', and reflection. They pay attention to group processes that promote collaboration and responsiveness.

Figure 4.4: *Inclusive leadership promotes a high learning frame*

Low learning frame	High learning frame
• Mistakes are crimes to be punished • I know it all • I don't need to learn from others • If you don't have a solution, don't raise the problem • If I'm uncomfortable something is wrong • Speaking up invites criticism • I'm powerless in this group so will be quiet	• Mistakes are puzzles to learn from • Other people may have information I lack • I can learn from others • It's helpful to raise problems even if I don't have a solution • I'll stick with the discussion even if I'm uncomfortable • I'll say what I think even though I may be criticised • I can make a contribution without formal authority

Learning also includes the 'meta-skill' of being able to reflect on and modify our embedded, automatic responses. Automatic responses block new ways of thinking and acting. Instead, with a high learning frame, individuals identify and reflect on their own interactions. They analyse them to understand how their unconscious, fast thinking might affect how they contribute in the team.

It is here that real value can come from training and awareness of unconscious bias. If we can stay curious about how our attitudes work, and how they get in the way of good decisions, we can overcome their impact on collective work.

A new script to beat bias

Here is an opportunity for Prime Minister Scott Morrison to demonstrate inclusive leadership. In his position as a national leader, he is a role model and people pay particular attention to what he says. What better person to make his messages more inclusive, acknowledging the greater gain to be had when we amplify everyone's talent and potential?

As Prime Minister of Australia, his obligation is to consider the welfare and prosperity of the country and *all* its constituents. He should focus purposefully on promoting win:win mind-sets. How could Australia be a better country? How could our institutions and businesses be more productive and successful into the future? By taking on a mindset that promotes diversity and showing how we *all* benefit from it. That will happen when we can *all* access it, and Scott Morrison can help us to do that.

Here's a suggested re-script:

> *We want to see women rise.... when women rise and contribute at their full potential, we all rise as a society. Everyone gains.*
>
> *[Equality] is about Australians appreciating the richness and diversity of our society. When we work together, we lift others up, we lift ourselves up. That's our values. That... you lift all the people up. And that is true about gender equality too. We need to open opportunities to both women and men, and that will make us stronger.*
>
> *Prosperity brings with it its opportunities, of course it does, for every person. As everybody grows in their contribution to our society, so do we as a society grow.*

To be more successful, we need to change workplace cultures away from emphasising masculine contest norms. We need to promote gender-inclusive norms. That requires the buy-in of men, particularly privileged men like Scott Morrison.

We tend to promote masculine, over-confident, narcissistic, psychopathic individuals into leadership positions.[10] We mistake masculine contest characteristics for leadership characteristics. Leaders with these characteristics advance their own careers, but they do not advance the work of the team, nor create a resource for the organisation.

Men and women can work together to change cultures so that they are more inclusive. When they are inclusive, they benefit everyone. Gains for women are also gains for men, and gains for society. For example, in countries that are higher in gender equality, both men and women win more Olympic medals. Research suggests this is because structural equality fosters conditions that allow all talent to reach its peak.[11] This is an apt metaphor for the approach of inclusive leadership.

Bias Buster 4

Celebrate gender inclusion

- ► Find and celebrate your role models for inclusive leadership.
- ► Help your organisation articulate what inclusive leadership is.
- ► Support leaders to develop their inclusive leadership capabilities.
- ► Create peer networks to encourage mutual support for inclusive leaders.
- ► Promote development and coaching programs to help leaders be more inclusive.
- ► Recognise inclusive leaders for their capabilities and achievements.

What to value: the benefits of diversity for your organisation's future

We should understand that diversity and inclusion are not 'something nice' to do in addition to our 'real work', but are central to mission success.

— CHARLES F. BOLDEN, JNR, NASA ADMINISTRATOR[1]

Who would have thought that the dinosaurs wouldn't be around forever? When whatever change it was hit the world, the dinosaurs weren't ready for it. They existed for millions of years and seemed solid enough to outlast pretty much anything, yet they couldn't pivot rapidly enough.

Does your organisation work in a fast-changing environment where non-routine work is increasingly common? If so, diversity of thought is fundamental to your future success. In the United States at least, almost all real job growth is occurring in non-routine cognitive work.[2] Product or service innovation, the rise of artificial intelligence, machine learning and making accurate predictions all need diversity. Non-routine cognitive work requires the ability to solve complex, unique problems and produce new knowledge. When it comes to such work, inclusive teams of diverse individuals outpace individuals working alone.

Without diversity, you won't pivot. Organisations won't be competitive into the future. They won't be able to innovate, adapt, or keep up with competitors and left-field entrants that don't even exist yet. Without it, like the dinosaurs, organisations face extinction.

Diversity and inclusion are fundamental to future organisational success.

Diverse people create diverse thinking

Much of the diversity work we've being doing for the last 50 years has been focused on how to get women into work, and at the leadership table. The involvement of women and African Americans accounted for 15 to 20 per cent of productivity growth between 1960 and 2008.[3] Even hard-nosed economists now identify the benefit of diverse workforces. Productivity in the developed world is plateauing[4], so on economic terms alone it makes a great deal of sense to involve people from diverse backgrounds to maximise the pool of available talent.

The ability of organisations to innovate and be commercially successful depends on people who have different ideas and perspectives.[5] That depends on having diverse thinking. Having diverse people is the easiest way to get diverse thinking.[6] Yet diversity isn't enough. Inclusion matters not just because it feels good or because it does good; inclusion turns diversity into value for your organisation. Diversity of thought is the gateway to innovation, and inclusion is the pathway.[7]

The difference between diversity and inclusion, and why it matters

One of the truisms to have entered the diversity conversation is that diversity always adds value. One 2019 headline proclaimed that 'the business case for diversity is now overwhelming'.[8] On the one hand there is some truth in the proclamation. As organisations become larger and more complex, they need new thinking and skills to meet the challenges they face. But we don't always need diversity to get the right outcomes and just having diversity in the room doesn't mean we gain from it.

Distinguished University Professor of Complexity, Social Science, and Management Scott C. Page sifts through a decade of evidence to identify under what circumstances diversity does yield a dividend.[9] Page found that one of the critical variables is whether a task or a project actually requires diversity of thought. If it's a routine task, diversity will almost certainly *interfere* with its achievement. Routine tasks where the focus is on efficiency to minimise costs of production are best performed by homogeneous groups. Organisations where work tasks are routine need efficiency, stability and control to be effective. The old hierarchical paradigm that values homogeneity is probably going to be more successful.[10]

To have value, cognitive diversity must be necessary to achieve the best outcome for the task.

By contrast, non-routine work or complex problem-solving, research, strategy, planning and prediction all need diversity. While routine tasks, like delivering parcels to homes, don't appear to benefit from diversity among drivers, the teams that create the complex algorithms that create the delivery routes do.

Diversity doesn't produce a benefit where tasks can be separated and completed by individuals. Smart individuals should be handed their tasks and allowed to get on with it. (It's a common mistake to create 'teams' and expect people to work together on everything when doing so causes a drop in productivity for the team.[11])

Complex tasks and opportunities require teams of cognitively diverse people to work together, and this is where the value of diversity lies. When people are formed into teams to work together, and told that inclusive action is in their self-interest, they are most likely to do better.

As we've seen, benefit isn't guaranteed because there's a diverse group of people in the room. Identity-diverse groups must overcome a series of hurdles, as outlined in Chapter 4, and that relies on inclusive leadership.

The diversity in the room needs to be the diversity required for the task. Random diversity, having diversity for its own sake, isn't productive. Simply piling on the difference doesn't add value.

Research shows that the diversity in groups can divide as easily as it can unite, as we saw in Chapter 4.[12] Also as discussed in Chapter 4, subgroups may create 'fault lines'[13] and these interfere with information sharing, and may create tension. When we talk about men and women, we draw attention to subgroups, which widens the fault lines and that's when the differences may create problems.

The introduction of women into male-dominated symphony orchestras was made possible only when blind auditions were held.[14] Initially, the increased presence of women decreased levels of satisfaction and social functioning: not the desired result. Yet once the proportion of women reached around 50 per cent, the initial dissatisfaction plateaued or reversed.

Knowing the value of your diversity dividend makes the effort of achieving it worthwhile.

Strategies and policies don't on their own change behaviour. What does change behaviour is helping people to believe that interacting across differences will have value for them. It's harder work to do, so its purpose needs to be clear and compelling. That's not something that can be imposed.[15] Inclusion needs to be seen as a value that will promote individual as well as organisational interests and prosperity.

How diversity creates value

Page discusses three different justifications for diversity and inclusion.[16] The first is the normative argument. It holds that diversity and inclusion policies seek to redress past wrongs to create a better future. The second is the need for greater demographic diversity as a market response, in order to better represent stakeholders. The third is to achieve a diversity bonus; that is, to achieve better performance from cognitively diverse groups on complex tasks.

I'm with Page when he argues that the compelling approach for organisations is the last of the three. The normative argument, which is affirmative action, is seen by many as personally costly. It requires trade-offs that are unpalatable to many. Arguing to people that they need to make a sacrifice from which others will gain is a hard sell. Most of us don't like to give up what we see as our gains to rebalance the playing field. When companies position inclusion efforts in this way, performance tends to decline.[17]

Page says that we should not focus on diversity and inclusion because it's the right thing to do.

In organisations we should focus on diversity because it is 'the sensible and innovative thing to do'.

The compelling logic for increased diversity is because it increases performance. There's no sacrifice required. Organisations exist to be successful, to make profits, or achieve particular outcomes. The purpose of diversity must be aligned with this to make sense to people. There must be a meaningful 'business case'. The logic applies in any organisation dealing with information and needing to do things differently to survive in the future.

From Page's analysis of the evidence base, diversity of people and different mental models improve:

- accuracy of predications
- problem-solving
- number and value of options and ideas generated
- critical thinking

- ► creativity
- ► ability to verify the truth.[18]

This doesn't mean that a diverse team will always produce the best results. It does mean that on complex tasks, a diverse team will usually outperform a team of smart, homogeneous individuals. Even within groups, there are large differences in cognitive diversity. One of the great benefits of an approach that focuses on inclusion is in being able to explore those differences.

Affinity bias means that we are likely to ignore intra-group differences and there's untapped opportunity here. There is diversity within demographic groups down to the individual level and that variety will have a positive benefit in areas such as education, finance, entertainment and health. Individuals' experiences in these areas contribute considerable insight to organisations.

According to Page, 'our identities influence what we value and deem worthy of our time and attention'. Even the decision about which problems to address requires an identity-diverse team. How do we know which problems have value?

'We must be inclusive in deciding our goals if we want to create effective, inclusive groups and teams to achieve them.'[19]

Many studies show substantial benefits from teamwork can be attributed to diversity. The widespread belief that scientific or artistic breakthroughs need individual genius doesn't wash.[20] Even some of the greats, like Raphael, Michelangelo and Einstein, had assistants. Famous collaborations like Jobs and Wozniak, Crick and Watson or Marie and Pierre Curie are more common than lone geniuses.

Identify your diversity dividend

The bonuses that come from diverse groups in financial services, such as 5 to 20 per cent improvement in forecasts, or 60 basis points in share prices, are significant. Identifying your diversity dividend means knowing the value that your organisation creates when it manages diverse teams well. What is the extra value that diversity does, or could, contribute to complex team tasks in your organisation?

There are three key areas that can be leveraged: strategy, operations and performance. Which of these you use will depend on the data you already have, your stakeholders, and how much time and capacity you have to crunch the numbers.

In 2016, Australian-headquartered mining company BHP committed to achieving gender balance. At that time, one in six employees was female. In February 2020, one in four were. Their most diverse and inclusive teams:

- delivered 67 per cent fewer recordable injuries
- reported a 21 per cent higher sense of pride
- had 28 per cent lower unplanned absences
- had a plan and schedule work delivery rate that was 11 per cent higher than others.[21]

In the strategy area, consider your context, your customers and your organisational capability. The following areas have already been shown to benefit from increased diversity:

- More than 85 per cent of corporate value creation relies on people, brand and intellectual property.[22]

- An increased ratio of women contributes to increased innovation.[23]

- Collective intelligence improves group performance by over 40 per cent[24], leading to productivity dividends of up to 60 per cent.[25]

- An increased ratio of women better matches the consumer base: in households up to 80 per cent of decisions are made by women.[26]

In the operations area, consider your people, your systems and your processes. Removing bias will have the biggest impact in the people area, and the suggested measures in Figure 5.1, over the page, focus on these.

In terms of performance, organisations with the highest commitment to gender equality outperform industry medians. In one research study, profits as a percentage of revenue were higher by 34 per cent, as a percentage of assets by 18 per cent and as a percentage of shareholder equity by 69 per cent in those organisations with the highest levels of commitment to equality.[27] What could the impact be in your organisation?

Where there's even a 10 per cent bias in the likelihood of earning a promotion, and 10 steps in the hierarchy, 90 per cent fewer women will get to the top. If this applies to your organisation, what does it cost you?

Excluding female academic mathematicians from career opportunities, or making careers less attractive to them, reduces capacity. In the abstract, if a woman with a capacity of 20 opts out because workplace culture is unwelcoming, and a man with a capacity of 16 takes her place, mathematics suffers.[28] A talent deficit is created.

More diversity means that there is a bigger talent pool and a broader range of problems might be solved. Complex problems such as modelling obesity patterns or rising opioid use benefit from cross-disciplinary teams. Diversity increases the range of knowledge and perspectives, because of the increased cognitive diversity.

Every second of every day, the global online seller Amazon ships more than 400 boxes at a cost of more than US$10 billion every year. It has multidisciplinary teams determining the size and shape of the boxes. Even a 3 per cent diversity dividend would mean $300 million in savings. What could your dividend be?

The Vermont Oxford Network is a consortium of more than a thousand neonatal intensive-care units sharing best practices. Many small improvements are contributed by network members and they add up to major advances in care practices. Their success in lowering neonatal mortality rates comes from an accumulation of all their efforts. What similar measures could you use in your organisation?

Figure 5.1 identifies strategy, operations and performance measures to value diversity for your organisation.

In summary, diversity of thinking comes from diverse people: they are the most efficient way to get it. Having diversity in the room isn't enough. You've got to work it to make it pay. The best teams have loads of it and the worst teams have loads of it. What makes the difference? Scott C. Page's analysis shows that when people with diverse cognitive abilities work inclusively on complex tasks there is a quantifiable benefit. Knowing what your bonus is, or could be, requires having the right measures to track progress.

Figure 5.1: Diversity dividend measures

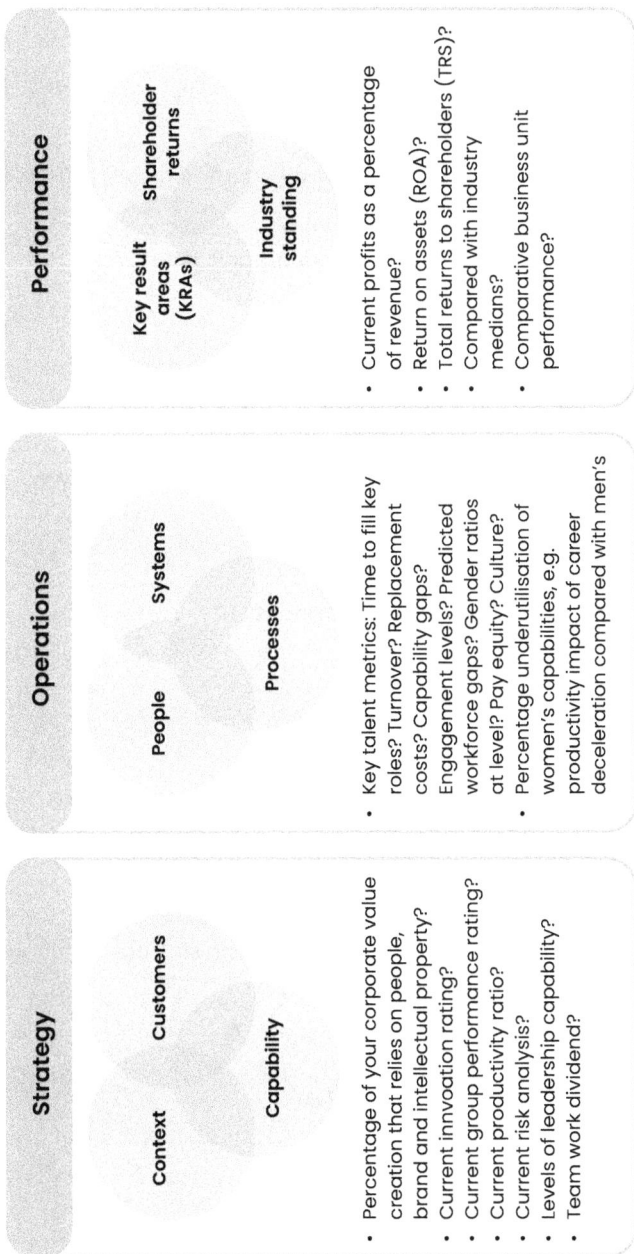

Strategy

Context   **Customers**

Capability

- Percentage of your corporate value creation that relies on people, brand and intellectual property?
- Current innovation rating?
- Current group performance rating?
- Current productivity ratio?
- Current risk analysis?
- Levels of leadership capability?
- Team work dividend?

Operations

People   **Systems**

Processes

- Key talent metrics: Time to fill key roles? Turnover? Replacement costs? Capability gaps? Engagement levels? Predicted workforce gaps? Gender ratios at level? Pay equity? Culture?
- Percentage underutilisation of women's capabilities, e.g. productivity impact of career deceleration compared with men's

Performance

Key result areas (KRAs)   **Shareholder returns**

Industry standing

- Current profits as a percentage of revenue?
- Return on assets (ROA)?
- Total returns to shareholders (TRS)?
- Compared with industry medians?
- Comparative business unit performance?

Bias Buster 5

Know your diversity dividend

Use these prompts to discover and communicate your diversity dividend.

- The future challenges for our organisation are...

- Our current performance, relative to industry standards is...

- The risks we face are...

- A key driver to improve performance and our standing against competitors is to increase innovation. Innovation increases market share (%). It leads to productivity improvements (%) which can be realised by...

- We currently:

  - underutilise existing capability (%)

  - lose good talent (%), and

  - fail to attract key necessary capabilities (opportunity cost).

- Group and team performance can be enhanced by increased diversity and good management, resulting in increases of (%).

- A better gender balance at the senior levels of our organisation (%), has the potential to shift our performance and results dramatically (%), by:

  - fully using our existing talent

  - keeping key talent, and

  - increasing our attractiveness as an employer of top talent.

PART II

Why your organisation isn't fair (even if you think it is)

We believe that we have superior access to the stuff inside our minds... It is hard for human beings, endowed with the capacity for conscious thought, to accept that the beliefs and preferences that so define us can be shaped by forces outside our awareness.

— MAHZARIN R. BANAJI & ANTHONY G. GREENWALD[1]

Working with conscious thought processes is challenging enough; working with the intangible unconscious and its distortions is even more so. Adding to the challenge is the perplexing fact that individuals often have conscious and unconscious beliefs that are contradictory. As mentioned in Chapter 2, what we know about unconscious bias and how it works is relatively new and the emerging insights that can inform practice are by no means definitive. It still feels a bit like 'stepping through the looking glass'.

How best to mitigate the effects of individuals' unconscious beliefs and improve decision-making? We can do this by understanding how these beliefs play out and influence decisions, then having clear strategies for mitigating them.

Unconscious bias hinders women's progress in organisations in three key ways:

1. **You can't be what you can't see.** Affinity bias constrains women's own choices, as well as organisational talent decisions. Chapter 6 recommends actions to take to minimise these constraints.

2. **You're damned if you do and doomed if you don't.** Women's progress is limited by powerful, invisible binds created through expectancy bias. Chapter 7 makes them transparent and suggests ways to overcome them.

3. **What you see is not what you get.** Confirmation bias distorts perception and reality about women's leadership potential and talent. Chapter 8 provides a guide to decode the connection and suggests tactics for increasing merit by being more systematic.

The biases and their impacts are shown in the diagram below.

Unconscious biases that hinder women's progress

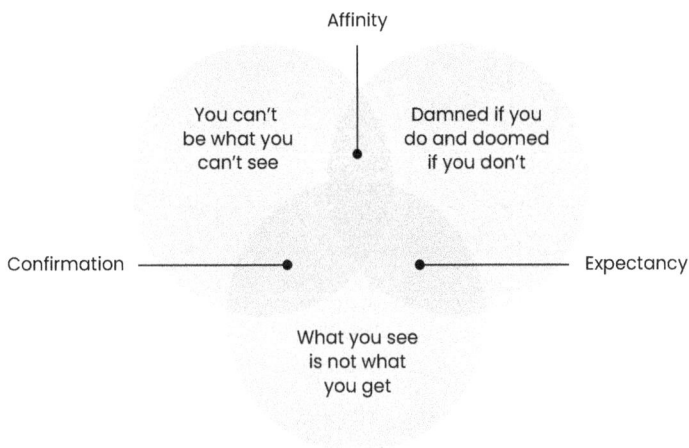

Affinity

You can't
be what you
can't see

Damned if you
do and doomed
if you don't

Confirmation ————————•   •———————— Expectancy

What you see
is not what
you get

Targeted organisational strategies counteract bias and improve talent decisions. This section provides key advice on organisational strategies that *do* work. It provides specific, practical strategies that will interrupt, reduce or bypass each of the biases. This provides you with the opportunity to improve your decision-making, as well as keep and grow your best talent.

The figure over the page summarises the relationship between helpful strategies to circumvent the three key biases:

► Make role models visible.

► Help women to belong in leadership.

► Systematise decisions to see true talent.

Three key tactics to reduce biases

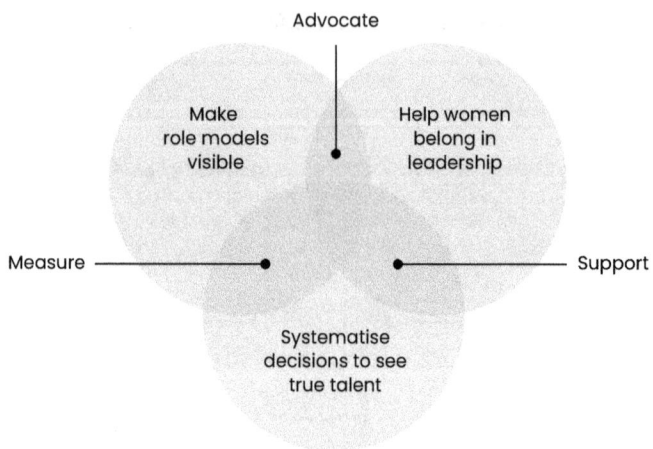

Advocate

Make
role models
visible

Help women
belong in
leadership

Measure

Support

Systematise
decisions to see
true talent

6

You can't be what you can't see

You can't be what you can't see.

— ATTRIBUTED TO MARIAN WRIGHT EDELMAN

When there are no female role models, women's belief in their suitability for leadership reduces.[1] The lack of female role models constrains the choices women make about their careers. In other words, there's an affinity bias: you can't be what you can't see.

Affinity bias stops women from seeing themselves as leaders

Affinity bias means that we like people who are just like us and are more influenced by them. I am more likely to emulate people like me than those not like me. This can have a significant impact on which careers we choose. If I can see 'people like me' in a particular occupation or job role, I'll choose that path. If I can't, if there's no-one in an occupation or job role who looks like me, I am less likely to choose it.

Girls are discouraged from pursuing careers that seem 'male'. Likewise, boys are discouraged from pursuing careers that seem 'female'.

This limits organisations' talent pools and pipelines, compromising long-term future talent supplies across industries. It is strikingly evident in male-dominated professions such as engineering.[2]

➕ The impact of affinity bias starts early

When she was 12 years old, my friend Grace decided that she wanted to be a scientist when she grew up. She believes that it is very important for girls to want and be able to be scientists. She thinks that if more girls did science, Australia's productivity would rise.

Grace was curious about why more girls don't do science; there were few in her class. True to her budding scientist tendencies, she conducted an experiment to try to find out more. She asked her own science class, and one at a similar school, to complete the Implicit Association Test.[3] The test measures the implicit associations we hold, in this case, about gender and science/humanities. Most people readily associate men with science and women with humanities. Even if we hold conscious egalitarian beliefs, most of us unconsciously maintain these traditional associations.

Grace was shocked to learn that most of her 12-year-old classmates had unconscious gender associations. Both boys and girls had implicit beliefs that boys do science and girls do humanities. She hadn't expected that to be the case.

One of the two schools had a special science program. Grace was relieved to find that the girls participating in that program saw themselves as being as good at science as the boys. Girls from the other school saw themselves as being half as good. She concluded that special science programs can help increase girls' confidence in their abilities.

Achieving balanced senior leadership in many organisations relies on qualifications in science, technology, engineering and maths (STEM). STEM qualifications facilitate access to important line and operational roles, and these roles are critical to the leadership pipeline in industries such as construction, mining, resources, logistics, infrastructure, science and research where there are currently few women.

Implicit gender associations affect whether girls are supported, encouraged and successful in STEM.

Here is a snapshot of the ways in which unconscious bias affects the decisions of girls, teachers, families and bosses. They explain why so few girls in Australia enrol in a tertiary science degree:

- As early as three years of age, boys and girls associate traditional gender roles with jobs (even in the 21st century).[4]

- Stereotypes about gender and job fit become engrained by the time a child is in primary school. Girls and boys have implicit beliefs that maths and science are for boys.[5]

- Parents have lower expectations for their daughters' STEM abilities than for their sons'.[6]

- Girls' efforts are attributed to hard work and conscientiousness, boys' to innate talent or brilliance.[7]

- Beliefs precede reductions in actual test scores; that is, even when girls score well at maths they don't believe they do.[8] Their maths scores fall away at around age 13.[9]

- In high school, teachers pay 39 per cent more attention to boys in science class, and describe boys as smart and curious.[10]

- Girls' academic self-beliefs and enrolment preferences move away from STEM in high school.[11]

- At university, women represent approximately 15 per cent of engineering and IT undergraduates.[12]

- Hirers prefer male candidates over female; they are seen as more worthy of mentoring and deserving of a higher salary.[13]

- Recommendations emphasise males' research skills, publications and careers. Females are recognised for teaching and practical clinical skills and for personal attributes.[14]

- Female researchers are less likely to receive grants.[15]

- During their careers, women report feeling isolated and excluded from informal social gatherings. They have less opportunity to collaborate with senior faculty. They receive inadequate professional mentoring.[16]

- Care-giving responsibilities affect women's careers more than men's. Inadequate childcare facilities, reduced travel and absence from conferences all affect opportunities.[17]

This may feel like a long litany of problems, and it is. Yet really it is just the same problem manifesting in many different ways. Central to the challenge is one issue: implicit or unconscious gender beliefs. Implicit beliefs affect decisions we make for our daughters, our sisters, our colleagues and ourselves.

How to break the link between men with careers, women with family, men with science and women with the humanities?

What could you do, if you were Grace's parent, teacher or friend, to help Grace pursue her dream of being a scientist?

You can enlighten yourself by knowing your own implicit beliefs. How do they influence what you do and how you decide, and how do your decisions affect the choices available to girls like Grace – and to those girls who by the time they are 12 have discounted a career in science? You can enlighten them by helping them understand how their own implicit beliefs affect them. Challenge anything that limits choice.

Girls are more likely to continue with science if female friends have performed well, or where there is collaborative learning.[18] When women are exposed to female role models, their implicit attitudes decrease and their positive identification with their field increases. They increase their efforts on difficult tests and feel more confident.[19] You can ensure Grace has access to supporters and role models. These include girls and women at all ages and career stages as they engage with science.

Stories about successful women in science and technology have value. The greatest value comes from role models who are accessible and with whom girls like Grace can directly interact. Positive relationships with role models inoculate girls against the negatives listed above. Find those role models. Encourage girls like Grace to pursue their dreams, watch your language and always stay positive. Girls can!

My friend Anna has run an engineering consulting firm with her husband for 30 years. As she says:

> When I was studying engineering in Poland, half the class were girls. I don't get it! I don't understand why there are so few girls doing science and engineering in Australia in the 21st century. I don't understand why it might be seen as

unusual that our three daughters are all scientists: a computer engineer, an environmental scientist and a medical practitioner. It should not be remarkable. It should just BE.

How implicit affinity bias affects women's own career choices

Implicit self-beliefs are not simply private thoughts that remain confined to the mind. Rather, they impact intentions and goals. They either encourage or hinder future professional success.

On entry to tertiary studies, and again on exit, young women agree that women-as-a-group are as suited to leadership roles as men. They express their own personal ambition to be leaders. However, their unconscious beliefs about women as leaders, and about their own leadership potential, do change. Without the right kind of interactions with role models, young women's implicit self-beliefs diminish.[20] When all or most of their professors are male, their unconscious self-beliefs are eroded.[21] They come to believe that women are better suited to support roles.

By contrast, when women directly engage with successful female professors, their unconscious self-beliefs improve. Frequent contact helps to strengthen the association 'woman = leader'. Only when contact is evaluated as meaningful – when a sense of similarity with role models is created by a meaningful, quality connection – do self-beliefs change: 'I can be a leader.' Thanks to the positive potential of affinity bias, women's leadership ambitions increase significantly when they engage with such role models.

The same pattern continues as women engage in the workforce[22], where they are less likely to pursue leadership roles and roles in masculine domains.

Young women are unaware of their implicit beliefs. They believe that the way they see themselves and their career choices are down to their own motivation, talent and interests. Instead, context powerfully drives their choices.

One senior leader described her daughter's reduced ambition as like the erosion caused by acid rain. She started her career as a confident, ambitious young woman. She was clear about who she was and what she wanted. Over time, she began to give up career goals and her dreams of success. One drop at a time, and devastatingly over time, her interest in her career was being eroded. She was shaping herself in line with expectations about what women should be like at work. Not confident. Not ambitious.

Before this information becomes too depressing, it's important to note some positives. While gender associations are still prevalent, the strength of them is reducing in younger groups. Sub-categories of women are becoming more common. For example, the sub-category of 'working women', is increasingly common.[23] There appear to be no matching shifts in associations between men and roles.

And it is becoming more common to see women as competent, although not as agentic.[24] In research published in 2019 that reviewed US opinion polls over 50 years, there was more acceptance that women are as smart as men but not that they are as ambitious. These indicators of consciously expressed attitudes are positive signs. Stereotypes may change. And as associations between gender and roles change at the conscious level, we can expect this to feed through to implicit attitudes as well.[25]

The ingredients that best predict improvement in implicit leadership self-beliefs are:

- knowing that other women have achieved success in leadership or male-dominated domains

- the experience of personally connecting with those women.

Chapter 3 discussed women whose leadership was as toxic as men's. Clearly, they are not the female leaders I have in mind as role models. Now seems a good time to confront the Queen Bee myth.

Forget Queen Bees – senior women support other women

Historically, successful women have attracted negative reactions that focus on their interpersonal capabilities[26], running the risk of being characterised as a Queen Bee, the 'quintessential bitch' who is concerned only with herself. Meryl Streep's character in *The Devil Wears Prada* is often used to illustrate the point. The supposed source of the character Streep portrays is Anna Wintour, described on her Wikipedia page as having an aloof and demanding personality, earning her the nickname 'Nuclear Wintour'.

While we are able to recognise this pattern, up-to-date research indicates that the sting does not come from women in senior roles.

But first: what is a Queen Bee? 'Queen Bee' is used to describe the 'bitch who stings other women if her power is threatened'. The term is used to blame senior women for not supporting other women.[27]

Where women are in a significant minority, there is enormous pressure to join with the majority group (men), and the power of that group is attractive. This causes 'insider' women to become hostile to 'outsider' women.[28] As a personal survival mechanism some women become as 'unwomanly' as possible and react with hostility to other women. They become part of the dominant group, sometimes taking on dominant group member characteristics and excluding other women. Queen Bees are seen to hold on to their power as the 'token woman'. They denigrate other women as 'emotional', express anti-female attitudes and avoid female-focused gatherings.

Such women, who perform well in male-gender-stereotyped roles, are generally not liked. They attract negative reactions that focus on their lack of warmth in particular. Both women and men see them as less desirable as bosses, compared with men described in the same way.

In 2016 research, C.L. Dezső and colleagues examined the under-representation of women in US S&P top 1500 firms over a 20-year period.[29] They found that the presence of one woman in the executive teams of these firms reduced rather than increased the chance that a second woman would be appointed to that team.

As that seemed so counter-intuitive, they explored the potential causes further. Was it Queen Bee practices that prevented a second woman getting into the top team? According to the Queen Bee profile, if the person with the top job is a woman, it should be less likely that another woman will be appointed to the top team. The reverse was in fact the case: a second woman was much more likely to be appointed to the top team if the *CEO was a woman*. In addition, firms appeared to hire women into senior management roles in response to actions by their female board members.

Where does the sting come from, then? The answer, the researchers suggest, is an 'implicit quota'. They argue that while firms gain legitimacy if they have women in top management, the marginal value they gain after one woman is appointed declines with each successive woman. The perceived costs, from the perspective of the male majority in top management, may increase with each woman. Therefore they are more likely to stop at one.

How to leverage the role-model effect to counteract affinity bias

Leveraging role models is the leadership action that breaks the paradox of 'You can't be what you can't see'. Visibility of women leaders creates a new norm of women as a good fit for leadership. CEOs and executive committees lead by engaging with senior women as colleagues. They advocate for gender-balanced leadership.

Increasing the number of women in key roles increases the availability of role models. It increases identification with leadership roles and it helps grow future supply.[30] A diversity of role models expands the leadership profile and boosts innovation.[31]

As seen above, the mere presence of women in small or 'token' numbers is not enough.[32] Achieving a critical mass of 35 per cent or more enables:

- ► supportive alliances to form between women, increasing their retention

- recognition of women for their individual talents, rather than for stereotypical attributes

- improved dynamics and culture of the larger leadership cohort.[33]

Make role models visible and accessible

Increasing girls' interest in male-dominated professions is critical to gender-balancing occupational pipelines. In some professions, this will take 10 to 20 years. There is a growing range of programs that support girls' engagement with science. Examples include STARportal online resources to inspire young people's interest in science and the AMSI Choosemaths program. The Athena SWAN program aims to help academic scientists' careers.

Young women are more likely to succeed when role models are present while they are studying and developing their careers. The role-model effect works when girls and young women engage with female peers, for example, those who are a year or two ahead of them at school or university and have STEM expertise.

Organisations can operate from the same principles. Make early-career women aware of the full range of career options, connect them with mentors and sponsors. Allow them to form peer groups to discuss these options, and this will help them move through the pipeline. If there are no 'local' role models, find them. One way to do that is by sharing stories of successful women. Being exposed to biographies of influential women has a similar, positive effect.

Harness the power of male advocacy

To achieve a critical mass of women in leadership, hiring patterns need to shift. The most powerful way for that to happen is by male leaders advocating for gender-balanced leadership.

+ The power of advocacy using storytelling

Chris Sutherland won the AHRI CEO Diversity Champion Award 2017 when he was CEO of Programmed. He was recognised for his ability to empower employees and demonstrate excellence in workforce diversity.

Early in their diversity program, leaders were alert to potential backlash. The board and executives were committed, and they wanted to ensure buy-in from the key middle manager stakeholder group, according to Melissa Donald, who was General Manager, Group Human Resources at the time.

One of Chris' key leadership actions was to write a letter to all staff to make it clear why he supported diversity. This message was repeated in the employee induction, in newsletters and other touchstone communications so that it was a consistent, continuing message.

His letter to staff told them why Programmed was undertaking the diversity program and what it meant to him to do so. The letter stated that he wanted the organisation to look like the communities they operated in (including gender, Indigenous and ethnicity). He clearly outlined what the business benefit was to the organisation: how it contributed to achieving the strategy. The letter explained the benefits of diversity of thought from teams that come from different backgrounds and experiences. It also explained that 'if our culture, systems and processes meant that we effectively only recruited from half the population then we are missing out on some of the best people'. He was very open that he was learning about diversity and inclusion, and committed to exploring new ideas.

According to Melissa, Chris appreciated that his messaging would have a significant impact on his workforce. He was very conscious of the power his messages had. He was deliberate in his approach.

The organisation used storytelling a lot to highlight what people were doing and what they were achieving. One of the tactics successfully used was to begin with small pilots. Those pilots then became stories, told through the voices of the staff involved. Success stories were added into Chris's messaging. In this way the messaging was real, and about doing real work. It wasn't about what head office was saying you should do, it was what your colleagues were doing and how it benefited them.

Melissa confirmed how much this clear and consistent messaging from the CEO and storytelling had shifted the way that staff engaged.

CEO advocacy is the primary driver of a rapid achievement of critical mass. Advocating pro-diversity views promotes acceptance of diversity and helps to realise its benefits. Advocacy by influential figures is persuasive, as we saw in Chapter 1. As CEOs and senior leaders are mostly men, their role as advocates is key.

The best ways men can champion gender equality are by:

- being credible, trustworthy supporters of gender-balanced leadership
- delivering well-articulated and congruent messages about gender balance and commitment to it[34]

- using persuasive power to change the minds of peers
- working collegiately with women.[35]

Because it is still uncommon to hear men advocate in this way, when they do, it stimulates a mental double take. It challenges unconscious thinking. Engaging senior men as advocates is also a positive way to tap into their desire to look good to others, to make a positive impression.[36] Once role models are present in an organisation, methods for meaningful engagement with them can be created.

Bias Buster 6

Make role models visible

To avoid 'You can't be what you can't see', leverage role models:

- Identify areas where there are no or few role models.
- Identify potential role models who are just one step senior to the women you have in your team.
- Create opportunities for them to meet and develop relationships around their work and experiences.
- If there are no internal role models, profile external women who have succeeded. Promote access to external women, arrange networking events and support women's attendance at external events.
- Ensure male leaders speak about the value of gender-inclusive leadership and sponsor junior women.
- Cross-cut difference. Find demographic connections between senior leaders and professionals such as culture, handedness and personality.

7

Damned if you do and doomed if you don't

As 'atypical leaders,' women are often perceived as going against the norms of leadership or those of femininity. Caught between impossible choices, those who try to conform to traditional – i.e., masculine – leadership behaviors are damned if they do, doomed if they don't.

—CATALYST[1]

Professor Nalini Joshi, a leading Australian mathematician, wore a casual cotton blouse when she addressed the National Press Club in 2016. She said that when she wears a business suit to such functions she is often mistaken for a member of the wait staff.[2] A woman is expected to be in a subservient position, not to be the headline speaker.

Women are commonly demoted to traditional gender roles.[3] Female doctors are often mistaken for nurses, female lawyers for paralegals and female professionals of many kinds for personal assistants. We do not expect women to hold senior roles, despite the fact that, increasingly, they do.

Women in organisations, including those in very senior positions, are expected to do the 'office housework'. In one study 45 per cent of women had been asked to make the tea in meetings. Singtel's CEO Chua Sock Koong speaks of frequently being mistaken for the secretary.[4]

In one of the organisations I consult to, emptying the dishwasher has become a symbol of gendered expectations. There, women complain about being the 'only one' to empty the dishwasher while men say, 'We didn't know we had a dishwasher.' That could be amusing if it wasn't for the unconscious biases that it masks.

Women want to be warm and helpful. Without even thinking about it, women will volunteer to do all sorts of tasks, from making the tea and taking the notes in meetings to supporting others to advance their careers. We expect women to do this work, and it is often invisible. When a man offers to help in these ways, we praise him for his contribution. His help is less expected and much more visible.

If a woman declines to help, she faces backlash; she's seen as selfish. When a man says no, there's no similar backlash; he must be busy.

While women help others out more, it benefits them less. Spending more time on office housework penalises women in two ways: it reinforces stereotypes about what we should expect from a woman, and time spent helping others means less time spent helping herself.[5]

We still expect men to be competent and women to be supportive. A recent European study reviewed 125 applications for venture capital funding[6] where women had applied for and received less funding. There were four distinct differences in the language used to assess applications:

1. Women were described as needing support, men as assertive.

2. Women were not described as entrepreneurs but as growing a business to escape unemployment. Superlatives were used about men's fit with entrepreneurship and risk-taking.

3. Women's credibility was questioned, men's was not.

4. Women were seen to lack competence, experience and knowledge; men to be innovative and impressive.

Expectations about how men and women should behave were carried over into evaluations and affected their relative success. Women are penalised when they move into domains seen as masculine.

How expectancy bias makes it a struggle for women to fit into leadership

Women struggle to fit in. They are often caught in the 'Damned if you do, doomed if you don't'[7] trap. They are caught between the need to be competent and assertive to receive respect as organisational leaders, and to be warm and nurturing to meet their 'appropriate' social role.[8] This is a consequence of the lack of role models as noted in Chapter 6 and the stereotype of leadership as male.

When it comes to leadership, we expect men to be ambitious and we don't expect women to be. This erodes women's ability to express their ambition. In many professions, from policing to medicine and science, women begin with the same levels of ambition as men. Yet, while men's ambition increases over time, women's decreases.[9]

Organisational researchers Williams and Tiedens suggest that women need 'to engage in corporate jujitsu in order to succeed as strong leaders'.[10] Relative to men, when women use dominance it hurts their likeability and hireability. While these findings were published in an article entitled 'The Subtle Suspension of Backlash', when the article was featured in Stanford's *Insights* newspaper it appeared with the headline, 'Can Women be Strong Leaders Without Being Labeled "Bossy"?' Apparently not. The article's title highlights how complicated it remains to connect women with agency and leading.

Because women are constantly fighting structural barriers, their ambition often wanes. And that keeps women's representation lower than it could be. 'Damned if you do and doomed if you don't', combined with 'You can't be what you can't see' is a potent mix to overcome.

Affirmative action has been one structural attempt to shift the numbers at the top and therefore loosen up some of the perceptions that surround what we expect of women. Studies led by organisational psychologist Professor Madeline Heilman between the mid-1980s and mid-2000s examined the impact on women hired under affirmative action policies. Women hired *and explicitly identified as being hired under affirmative action programs* were generally seen to be less competent and less deserving of their positions.[11] This applied even where it could be demonstrated that they were *as competent and qualified* as male colleagues. (It's something of a conundrum that women as competent and qualified as male candidates had to be hired this way.)

Both men and women assessed the women described in this way as less capable. Women appointed through these processes held those views themselves, even when evidence of their competence was clear. They also went on to take less credit for successful outcomes and showed less interest in continuing in their leadership roles.

Recent analysis creates a more refined view that points to a fundamental problem with how we see affirmative action. Affirmative action is designed to ensure that equality of opportunity exists. It recognises that women and men of equal talent and skill tend not to be appointed to roles with the same frequency. If equality doesn't exist, we need to take the right steps to end barriers to achieving it.

A more refined view highlights the importance of the language we use. In a study on affirmative action quotas, Management professor Miguel Unzueta et al. found that women's self-image benefited from affirmative action, so long as they did not think they had *personally* benefited.[12] Other studies have shown that those who benefit from affirmative action do recognise the success of such policies. They see them as providing them with opportunities and they enjoy working for employers with affirmative action policies.[13] Where women are told their qualifications are high, they do not experience the same negative effects.

Stigma may well occur under certain conditions, and how women's success is described is a critical factor. If women are told they have won their role solely because they are women, they are more likely to feel stigma. Where women are told they have won their role because they are competent and capable, whatever the affirmative action landscape, there appears to be no stigma. (This happens not just for women but for any minority group. Male nurses working in a female working environment feel the same.)

It is highly unlikely that women will be placed in roles solely because they are women.

As long as women aren't described as winning roles *because* they are women, stigma is avoided.

As leaders, women operate in a domain that remains stubbornly outside of gender prescriptions. Because of this they experience a series of binds, as follows:

- Women leaders continue to face the Goldilocks dilemma: they are usually seen as 'too tough' or 'too soft', less frequently as 'just right'. The need to display 'competence' is associated with leadership, seen as a male attribute. It's when women act in line with female stereotypes that they're seen as too soft and not leadership material. The need to display dominance is associated with leadership and traditionally seen as a male attribute. When women express dominance directly, they are seen as unlikeable. When women act in ways that are inconsistent with female stereotypes they're considered unfeminine.[14]

► Women who put themselves forward for promotional opportunities may be seen as 'pushy' or 'aggressive'. Men are seen as 'go-getters' and 'straight shooters' when they do. If women are seen as too tough, they are seen as unlikeable and less confident and are less likely to be hired.[15]

► Women face the bind of having to meet higher standards but receive lower rewards. Even in situations where male and female leaders are assessed as having the same leadership capability, men receive higher ratings for performance and potential.[16] Women keep having to prove that they are leadership material because of the perceived 'lack of fit'. Women receive less feedback on their leadership[17], even though, when they do, they are more likely than men to adjust their behaviour.[18]

► Women attribute setbacks internally and men externally. For example, women are more likely to conclude, 'I knew I wasn't good enough', whereas men attribute setbacks externally, with statements like, 'This is a tough job.' Strangely, this flips for success. Women tend to attribute success to external factors such as luck and men tend to attribute it to their own capabilities.[19]

Because they're the right fit, men are more likely than women to be promoted two levels while women are more likely to make lateral moves. Men are more likely to have sponsors, who focus on their career advancement. Men are more likely to have high-profile assignments and line-management roles, both of which are pathways to the C-suite.[20]

To be seen as effective leaders, women must negotiate complex expectations across both female and male characteristics.

The degree of vigilance and attention to their impact on others is high.[21] Identity threat results. Women don't feel like they are the right fit, they feel inferior and they expect to be treated poorly as leaders.[22]

How to avert the struggle and help women belong in leadership

To break through these binds, organisations need to re-imagine careers and talent. Women belong in leadership. The evidence about capability says so. Yet they don't feel like they do.

To date, much of the responsibility for career advancement has rested with individuals. Women are still advised to 'lean in'.[23] This advice is ill-advised. For a start, career advancement is not as easy as it seems, given the lack of role models, the binds that women face and the impact of identity threat. If it encourages women to take on more masculine traits to be noticed, we're not doing anywhere near enough to fix the system.

If anyone should be 'leaning in', it is organisations. Organisations need to have the best possible talent so they can achieve the best possible outcomes. They should be seeking out talent, not waiting for it to surface in front of them.

Keeping the burden of responsibility for career progress with women is a symptom of unconscious bias and women must be relieved of this burden.

If your organisation has few role models at senior levels, there are still ways to promote the value of gender diversity. What it takes, according to Melissa Donald, is a 'partnership mindset'.

Review the requirements that employee groups, customer advocacy groups or supply chain partners have for increasing gender diversity. For example, government and other organisations have requirements for representation built into tender processes. To win their business, you need to show what you are doing to increase diversity. If you socialise these needs back to key leaders within your organisation, you can help to promote the value of action to help women belong in leadership.

Some organisations are working with their partners up and down their supply chains to leverage the work they are each doing. This helps to show the value to the business, to express the requirement for gender-inclusive leadership in business terms.

Industry organisations like the Business Council of Australia, Australian Industry Group and Australian Chamber organisations promote the value of gender diversity. These sources help to reinforce the value of women in leadership so that managers are more likely to welcome women into leadership roles.

Managers reduce identity threat and increase motivation to lead for women by:

- providing them with access to role models, advocating for diversity and telling stories about women leaders
- increasing awareness of how unconscious bias affects decision-making
- encouraging women to see themselves as leaders
- making them feel welcome in leadership roles
- being fair when they allocate office housework tasks

- recognising the contribution that office housework makes to the team's wellbeing

- promoting a gender-inclusive perspective of leadership.

Leaders (particularly male) persuade people to see leadership, and talent, without gender blinkers. They take the demographics out of talent decisions, focusing on capability. They move the onus for talent identification and growth from women to managers.

Acknowledging biases and replacing intuition with good processes allows careers to be reconceived. Therefore, organisations' talent systems can be adjusted to:

- review all recruitment, promotion and talent data to identify gender differences; rebalance where necessary

- experiment with gender-blind practices where disparities are identified

- ensure that equal role opportunities and equal pay are provided at entry level

- promote the value of leadership roles for women

- ensure mentors and supporters are provided to women in male-dominated professions and areas

- track the progress paths and progression rates of women and benchmark against men's.

Individual women can't shift these discrepancies; it is organisations that have the power to. They need to show how to make these changes, then reinforce managerial responsibility for fair talent and career management.

Bias Buster 7

Help women belong in leadership

- ► Create a clear description of what it means to be a good leader.

- ► Align leadership development, selection and promotion practices with the leadership description.

- ► Support women by providing sponsors, networks and role models. Help them connect. Find people who will actively support the career advancement of early-career women.

- ► Make sure sponsors know how to sponsor, and mentors know how to mentor in ways that will advance careers.

8

What you see is not what you get

Without systematic monitoring,
one can maintain the fiction of a meritocracy
but will have difficulty establishing and
sustaining a true meritocracy.

— FAYE CROSBY ET AL[1]

Recall the senior leader I referred to in Chapter 6, whose daughter's experience of gender prescriptions had the cumulative effect of acid rain. A drop at a time, but it was devastating over time, and her confidence eroded. Confidence remains a common feature in the discourse about women, ambition, careers and leadership. Our usual solution, as it was in this case, is to encourage or exhort women to 'be confident'.

Women's confidence is not the issue we should be talking about. Confirmation bias is.

Women do not lack a 'confidence' gene. They don't suffer from an inability to develop confidence skills, nor are they unable to develop a confident attitude. The senior leader's story highlights that women may be confident to begin with, but in the work environment they learn to moderate their confidence, or have it moderated!

How confirmation bias distorts our ability to spot leadership talent

Confidence runs directly counter to being feminine: to being submissive, kind and gentle. The female stereotype sees women as being better at support roles than leadership roles; they should not be confident of their ability to be a leader.

Our stereotypes influence our perceptions of others, causing us to view people in stereotype-consistent ways. They also influence our behaviour, leading us to interact with others in ways that elicit stereotype-consistent behaviour from them. They are both descriptive and prescriptive. If we believe that women are not confident, then we will notice elements of a lack of confidence when we interact with women. In social settings, information is often ambiguous and we can interpret it in different ways. We tend to use our stereotypes to guide our inferences. We tend to focus on the information that confirms the stereotype and we ignore or misinterpret information that contradicts it.

People are much better at recalling information that is stereotype-consistent. For example, having observed a group of six, they are more likely to recall and tell the story of the one woman who wasn't confident than of the five who were.

If we hold the general belief that women lack confidence, then we behave towards them as if they were not confident.

Women themselves learn not to display confidence. 'Damned if you do, doomed if you don't' is at work here too.

Consider this research:[2]

- In one experiment, female job applicants were divided into two groups. One group was told that their male interviewer had traditional views about women; the other that the male interviewer had non-traditional views. Women in the first group downplayed their ambitions and behaved much more femininely during the interview. Those interviewed in the non-traditional cohort behaved in less traditional ways.

- In a similar experiment, women performed poorly on intelligence tasks, to downplay their competence.

- In yet another, women behaved more stereotypically with men who had power over them.

Anticipating the expectations of others can shape behaviour in line with stereotypes. As with all stereotypes, they may be conscious, which makes it easier to become aware of them. Or they may be implicit, in which case we are unlikely to be aware when they are affecting our perceptions and behaviour. What women at work experience is a double bind that arises from confirmation bias. Leaders need to appear confident, yet women understand that looking confident runs counter to stereotypical expectations.

If you mistake confidence for competence you get incompetence

Let's explore the whole confidence–competence conundrum in more detail. Tomas Chamorro-Premuzic's analysis of the conundrum is enlightening.[3] Competence is how good *you are* at something. Confidence is how good *you think you are* at something. How accurate are people at assessing their own competence? Not very, it seems. A study of over 20,000 people compared their self-rated intelligence with actual scores and found less than 10 per cent overlap.[4] The same results have been found in studies of other competencies, such as academic performance and social skills.

Even more striking, those most lacking in competence make the least accurate evaluations of their talents. Most people overrate themselves in many ways, including their job performance.

The most competent people tend to underestimate their expertise. This suggests that the more you know, the more aware you become of how much there is to know.

Leaders who appear confident, regardless of their competence, can be very convincing. Overconfidence is infectious. If you say you are successful, people believe you; and because they believe you, they will work harder to ensure your success. It can sometimes lead to real success, not just the perception of it.

Someone may appear confident, but that doesn't mean that they feel confident. And the reverse, someone appearing unconfident doesn't mean they feel it. Someone who expresses doubts and identifies potential gaps may in fact voice those because they are confident.

We mistake the expression of doubt for a lack of confidence.

Both men and women exaggerate their ability, but men do it to a greater extent – about double the rate of women. On the basis of the exaggeration, men are more likely to be chosen for leadership roles. In one study, the penalty for women was that they were 30 per cent less likely to be chosen.[5]

It is a wiser decision to rely on unconfident, competent individuals. They prepare more for leadership roles, are more cautious and look for risks and obstacles, which improves their performance. Overconfident incompetence is more likely to be hidden – until it's too late.

Part of the bind is that competence and confidence are associated with men and not with women, as part of stereotypical gender schema. Yet many research studies have shown no gender differences in actual confidence levels. One review of more than 200 studies that Chamorro-Premuzic describes found that differences in confidence between men and women were negligible in adulthood. The same goes for a study of hundreds of European engineers. The difference found in the research is that while both men and women report feeling confident, it's how they are seen by others that differs. Women's self-confidence was reported *by others* as lower than when reported by the women themselves.[6]

In the female engineers' study, appearing confident didn't benefit perceptions others held of their leadership influence. Yet, it did have a benefit for men.

For women to be seen as influential leadership material, they need to be seen as confident and competent (masculine traits) and caring (a female trait). Men need to be seen only as confident.

Certainty bias erodes merit

Even if women are as confident as men, it is not enough to ensure their equal access to leadership roles. While equal amounts of confidence might mitigate confirmation bias, it doesn't mitigate certainty bias.

Our bias for certainty means that we tend to think that our decisions are much better than they are. So, we are not actually very likely to think we are biased.[7] It's a Catch-22.

Seventy-five per cent of HR leaders from top global companies say that the subjective opinion of the person's boss is the most common way to identify leadership potential.[8] And although many organisations spend a great deal of time identifying potential, they rarely check if they were right. Rather, they rely on selecting leaders based on instinct and intuition. In general, we believe that we are very good at choosing talent, yet without systematic processes it is most likely that unconscious bias undermines leadership selection. Leadership selection and succession needs to be re-tuned to focus on actual performance, not individual career success.

Admit you don't know, rather than you do

The most practical approach to avoiding certainty bias is to be aware of the tendency towards certainty. At an individual level, part of the work is to accept your own fallibility.[9] Frustratingly, because the biases operate unconsciously, we can't know when we are in their grip. Be more modest, less certain, about your decisions. Whether *you know you are biased* matters less than accepting that *you are likely to be biased*.

Leaders who play the 'merit card' probably suffer certainty bias: they don't think they are biased. They don't like the suggestion that they have a 'weakness' such as 'bias' and without that openness their decisions remain narrow. When we feel *most* certain we are most likely to be unsystematic. When we think we know, we circumvent objective methods or neglect to ask for alternatives.[10] If you accept that you are likely to be biased, you are more likely to act to mitigate bias. And that, currently, seems to get the best results.

Being less certain avoids the erosion of merit

Researchers Emilio Castilla and Stephen Benard found a 'paradox of meritocracy'. 'When an organisational culture promotes meritocracy (compared with when it does not),' they reported, 'managers... may ironically show greater bias in favor of men over equally performing women.'[11] When an organisation promoted itself as a meritocracy, managers awarded males more pay than they did females with identical performance ratings.

When merit is promoted as a cultural value, managers appear to become more confident that their decisions are impartial. Certainty bias creeps in. They invest less effort in avoiding the application of stereotypes, thereby creating the paradox. In these circumstances, managers' unconscious stereotypes are more likely to be triggered. Their pay decisions become *less* fair.

Even where ostensibly fair processes are set up, the results can be biased. In the venture capital funding application process referred to in Chapter 7, everyone on the panel was attuned to gender bias. They believed they weren't biased. Yet the researchers concluded that the questions that were asked *undermined* women's potential, but *underpinned* men's.[12]

A recent US study found a similar kind of bias. In a start-up funding competition, venture capitalists asked male entrepreneurs promotion-oriented questions. They focused on ideals, achievements and advancement. By contrast, they asked female entrepreneurs prevention-oriented questions. These questions focused on vigilance, responsibility, risk and safety. Male-led start-ups raised five times the funding of those led by females.[13]

Male and female venture capitalists displayed the same questioning biases. It is often assumed that men favour men and women favour women; increasing the number of women on selection panels is routinely seen as a good solution. Yet unconscious biases about gender are held as commonly by women as by men.[14] Increasing the number of female decision-makers does make balanced decision-making more likely, but it doesn't guarantee it. It is when panels have gender balance, or are female only, that bias tends to disappear.[15]

When decision-makers know that their decisions are being scrutinised for fair decisions, the fairness of their decisions increases. Organisations are more likely to be meritocracies where accountabilities are in place. That is, where:

- there are process accountabilities that clarify responsibilities and criteria for people decisions
- managers are accountable for the fairness of their decisions and results, and
- designated forums review people-management processes, decisions and criteria.

These tactics all reduce the likelihood of certainty bias.

How to make better talent decisions by being less certain, more systematic

To make better talent decisions, we need to be better at identifying talent. That means avoiding confirmation and certainty biases.

We can learn so much from following the research. I've explored the research to better understand how biases impact how we see women, confidence and competence, which in turn affects how we assess their merit for leadership. That enables us to substitute evidence for inference. It opens up new lines of inquiry.

Start with the right data

When we have the data, we can understand, in new and better ways, what's going on. And we can also seek to make change, if we choose to. If we keep measuring, we'll know what we have changed and when.

Discrimination between different demographic groups isn't always visible, so it may not be noticed at the individual level or within departments in the same organisation. Even those who are aware that such discrepancies occur may not notice them. According to social psychologist Faye Crosby, people notice persistent imbalances when they have systematic comparative data. Reviewing data that compares small groups across a larger collection – for example, departments within a larger organisation – shows different hiring patterns.[16]

Crosby and her colleagues put this down to a human need to believe that we live in a just world. When we perceive difference, we would rather put it down to a random quirk. That suits better than seeing deliberate discrimination. So we miss the patterns. Biased practices are not easily observable: they might be happening but you won't automatically recognise that they are.

Observers are not always able to detect unfairness in processes and that is why a valid assessment of the merits of women is harder to achieve than a valid assessment of the merits of men. Research confirms that, where men's capabilities and experiences are the same as women's, men are nevertheless more likely than women to be hired[17] and paid more.

Raters believe they make equitable judgements about individuals. However, assessments include subjective elements. The testing community admits that it is challenging to make fair assessments of individuals. Test construction and conditions remain open to bias. Measures give the appearance of objectivity, but don't guarantee it. Because we have used 'objective' assessment, we believe we have counteracted bias.

Implicit beliefs that associate men with leadership and women with support roles are held at least slightly by most people.[18] It is clear that even those of us with good intentions may not be able to avoid these when we are defining and assessing capability. To improve transparency we need to do two things: collect and report on the right data, and delegate accountability to address identified discrepancies.

Marc Benioff, CEO of Salesforce, pledged to create equal pay in his organisation. He believed that pay *was* equal, until he saw the data. An initial review of salaries in 2015 identified inequity in 6 per cent of salaries. In 2017, the same process was undertaken, due to company acquisitions.[19] Pay again had to be adjusted. Catherine Tanna, managing director of EnergyAustralia, implemented equal pay for doing the same job within her organisation in 2018.[20] She said it was not about gender; it was about fairness. And as Marc Benioff says, all CEOs have to do is press a button and they get the data. Measures are important, and continuing to pay attention to the data is as important.

Even when managers commit to promoting more women into leadership, they are prone to evaluate them less positively.[21]

Fair decisions can be made easier by analysing and structuring how information is conveyed and options are presented.[22]

Organisations are increasingly seeking to debias evaluation by using blind, automated processes. While automations rely on human programming and debiasing them is not without problems, such processes *can* minimise bias, resulting in better decisions.

Johnson & Johnson, which fields about 1 million job applications for over 25,000 job openings each year, now uses Textio, an automated writing service, to debias their job ads. Before they started using the service, they found that their job ads were skewed with masculine language. They were disproportionately valuing male characteristics. Their pilot program to change the language in their ads resulted in a 9 per cent increase in female applicants.[23]

Establishing measures provides a starting point and a finishing line: the scene is set. Recruiting and employing a diverse workforce is a necessary next step.

The challenge for those who don't yet get it is to agree to the overarching purpose that people decisions be based on merit. If merit is what we are aiming for, we should all be prepared to sign up for practices and tools that increase and uphold it.

Merit is both more and less than it seems; it is more complex and difficult to define than most people think. It is less objective and rigorous, particularly in knowledge work and leadership roles. It is ripe for bias.

Paradoxically, invoking merit is perhaps the most powerful way to subvert it.

If leaders admit to fallibility and are aware that they notice and value different people in different ways, there's plenty that can be done. There are many practices that will minimise bias and help make decisions fairer. We can all keep working to debias our decisions.

Measures are the 'hard' drivers of cultural change and inclusive behaviours are the 'soft'. Leaders promote inclusive behaviour by paying attention to growing a culture that supports inclusion. They call out exceptions, recognise exemplars, and circumvent the challenges of 'merit'. Focusing on inclusion means that a merit-based system can flourish. What you see will be what you get.

Reimagining what talent looks like can be reinforced through management systems. Data analytics surface patterns of advantage and disadvantage. Leaders authorise meaningful measures and they hold themselves to account for the fairness and quality of their decisions.

To improve transparency and drive new practices, managers should:

- clarify responsibilities and criteria for people decisions
- authorise the right measures

- hold managers to account for the fairness of their decisions

- hold regular forums to scrutinise and review decisions.

Bias Buster 8

Systematise decisions to see true talent

- Collect and use data for talent decisions.

- Watch out for confirmation bias.

- Accept your fallibility – be more modest, less certain about your decisions.

- Put the value back into evaluation – by using blind processes and ensuring scrutiny of outcomes.

PART III

The right culture to achieve gender balance

Our success as a society depends on all of us being able to reach our full potential – that's what gender equality is all about. Diversity is also essential to the success of our business because diversity of thought, background and perspective lead to better ideas for our clients and a more inclusive workplace for our people.

— LUKE SAYERS[1]

Talk about gender-balanced, open, inclusive cultures is now more prevalent. But we know that talk is cheap. To achieve gender balance we need to change the masculinity of work cultures.

Parts I and II of this book have identified what needs to change and provided insights at the local level for change. This section focuses on organisational culture as an important lever to get systematic and lasting change. Culture is hard to change, and culture that is informed by implicit attitudes that pervade society is even harder to change.

The challenges we face include:

- **What do we want to change?** We need clarity of focus about what the culture is now, and what we aspire to. As we better understand the difference between diversity and inclusion, the lens here is starting to sharpen.

- **What's the benefit of change?** There are still plenty of people who don't see the value of diversity. We need to keep articulating the value of difference to reduce backlash.

- **What does it take to make change happen?** Change is complex. Organisational culture change requires leadership engagement and persistence over a three- to five-year period.

Chapter 9 shows how to tackle cultural change. It identifies how to focus at the cultural level, articulate the benefits to everyone, and take steps to change culture.

9

Bring your legacy intentions to life through culture

Cultural norms define what is encouraged, discouraged, accepted, or rejected within a group. When properly aligned with personal values, drives, and needs, culture can unleash tremendous amounts of energy toward a shared purpose and foster an organization's capacity to thrive.

— BORIS GROYSBERG ET AL.[1]

It is in an organisation's culture that leadership intentions come to life. Nick Marinelli of Fulton Hogan Australia had a clear legacy intention to create a sustainable, gender-balanced organisation. He knew this meant embedding it in the organisation's DNA.

A committed leadership approach means providing strategic guidance to the cultural life of the organisation.

Organisational cultures can be adapted away from traditional gender scripts. There needs to be a reorientation away from proving masculinity. Compelling, inclusive behaviours need to be aligned with strategy. For both men and women. If the organisation's stories are always about feats of bravery or strength, masculine traditions are maintained. They need to be moderated by stories of compassion, learning or vulnerability. To achieve your legacy means understanding how to moderate masculine contest behaviours. Balanced, high competence, caring cultures attract highly talented individuals.[2]

+ A compelling case for culture change

When in 2017 Ingrid Bakker chose to guide HASSELL's gender-diversity approach from general commitment to strategic action, its culture was a foundation stone for its success.

Ingrid recalls that when she joined the board of the international design practice, there was already a general commitment to diversity.

In 2015, CEO Gerard Corcoran had become a member of the Australian Institute of Architects' Male Champions of Change program. That helped to get things started. Focus groups were held for men and women. They provided an idea of what needed to be done, but not necessarily who would do what.

By 2017, there was a sense that it was 'too big'. Diversity seemed to be everything. Coupled with that was a feeling that they were probably doing reasonably well. There was no particular focus for change. Ingrid saw a good opportunity to take the groundwork forward through a clear strategy and actionable initiatives. They needed to show *how* to convert the talk into action.

The first thing Ingrid considered was what to call their strategy. Labelling their focus 'gender balance' was important. 'Women aren't a minority', she says. 'We don't want to treat them like they are. The name should reflect their presence, and the goal.' For her, a focus on gender balance creates a different kind of conversation.

Ingrid worked with the Head of People & Culture, Emma Britton, to develop a strategy proposal for the board. The numbers were crunched as part of developing the gender balance strategy. Gender breakdowns for each of their professional groups was mapped, at each level of seniority. Their graduate intake ratio for Architects was balanced. From Associate level, the proportion declined at each of four steps up to Equity Partner, where it was 13 per cent.

During the board's discussion, this question was asked: 'How long will it take to get to 50:50 given existing numbers of staff at each level, and at the current progress rate?' The answer was 100 years! The board didn't find that acceptable. They decided to focus on fixing the pipeline in a series of stages, to remove the skew from the talent pool.

Since then, Associate representation has increased from the high 30s to 40 per cent. This is expected to cascade up to Senior Associate level in the next three years, then to Non-equity Partner in the following three years, and in a further three years to Equity Partner.

By focusing on the pipeline and fixing its skew, they have reduced the anticipated time to reach gender balance from a century to a decade. While they like to grow and promote their people from within, to fix the skew in this timeframe means that they will increase external recruitment.

Overall, there was strong board support for the strategy and the initiatives. The board saw the support and focus on gender balance as core to their culture.

The importance of culture

I asked Ingrid why there was such fertile ground for an explicit strategy on achieving gender balance. While it might be difficult to be definitive about cause and effect, HASSELL's existing culture seemed to be one that supported, in fact rested on, an explicit emphasis on diversity.

At the same time that HASSELL embarked on a new gender balance strategy, they also began reviewing their brand and culture. As I spoke with Ingrid, the HASSELL rebrand was being launched. This provides an unexpectedly detailed insight into the connection between their gender balance strategy and the essence of their culture as reflected in their brand.

They have four brand pillars: insight, creativity, inclusion and accountability. They take a multidisciplinary approach to their work that relies on a mix of skills and perspectives. The brand is underpinned by an ambitious culture where purposeful learning leads to great outcomes for clients – and everyone cares.

What stands out is how diversity is woven through the levels of their brand and culture approach. Threads of learning, insight, creativity, collaboration and inclusion lock diversity of thinking in as fundamental to their work.

Ingrid reflects that how HASSELL works is different to that of some other design firms. There is a clear intent to collaborate. The value of diversity of thinking and work, taking a multidisciplinary approach, is key. Everyone can be a part of the decision-making process and promote ideas. Valuing difference has always been a part of their DNA.

When benchmarked against other organisations, HASSELL achieves an 80 per cent engagement score, which is outstanding. People enjoy working there.

Strategy and culture are two primary levers for organisational effectiveness. Strategy offers a formal logic that orients people, while culture guides activity through shared beliefs and norms.[3]

HASSELL's focus on having a strong cultural context for diversity made the purpose of its gender strategy crystal clear. Similarly, when the diversity program was clearly integrated with the Fulton Hogan Australia strategy, it oriented people around its purpose. When diversity makes sense, when they know why, people will sign on.

How can you increase gender balance in your culture?

A focus on four areas will support culture change. The areas balance strategy with actions and guidance with support (see Figure 9.1, over the page).

Without leadership commitment, nothing happens. Leadership commitment gives purpose to, and guides clarity about, what needs to be done. HASSELL's strategy was based on an analysis of where gender balance was lacking. Their 16 initiatives identified clear actions to be taken that would improve the gender balance of their culture.

Coaching by top leaders cascades day-to-day support for gender-balanced action throughout the organisation. Some of HASSELL's actions were obvious, once the data was produced; it was a matter of making sure they happened. In other areas, HASSELL has provided development for leaders so that they understand what to do.

Consistency by leaders sustains change, makes sure the strategy is achieved and helps to keep a focus on what's next.

It's the way to embed the 'new normal'. Two years down the track at HASSELL, the brand and culture refresh shows the benefit of their consistency. Their gender balance strategy was enabled by their existing culture and is now in turn an enabler of their refreshed brand. The consistency is mutually reinforcing.

Figure 9.1: Levers for gender-balanced culture change

Committed leadership drives culture

What do leaders do and say? That's what culture is. And that's how people judge leaders' commitment to achieving a gender-balanced culture.

It's critical that leaders are committed to strategies for achieving better balanced cultures. If they aren't – if a leader's actions don't match their words – people will either blindly follow what they do or will be confused. They'll be disappointed if they believe in balance and will feel vindicated if they don't. If it's senior leaders who drive and reinforce a contest culture, they're first on the change agenda.

The power of lived experience

A CEO in the infrastructure industry sought advice about how to influence his most senior leaders; all of them had varying motivations. His personal motivation wasn't providing the spark to engage them.

The leader of the largest part of the business was seen as particularly resistant. I asked him about his own experience of diversity. He related a compelling story about working in a multidisciplinary team that had been a pleasure to be a part of. I then asked him to articulate why he thought diversity was important to him and to his business. Starting from a position of 'You have to do this because the CEO said so' didn't work for him! Finding a real story in his own experience triggered positive emotions. From there we could identify his own sense of purpose and how that fitted with what the CEO wanted to achieve.

Later, at a strategy workshop for all of the organisation's general managers, he retold his story. The power of someone labelled as resistant getting up and talking about why diversity had value was high.

At that same workshop, five different leaders shared their 'why' story. Each story was different and each was compelling. Together they provided a clear signal to the general manager cohort that this is important. But they didn't do it in a 'cookie-cutter' way. As lived, real experiences, the stories generated an honest, emotional connection with most of those present. It's fair to say that not everyone got it. But not everyone has to get it for progress to be made.

Culture can be somewhat opaque. To make it more transparent, I encourage leaders to use storytelling to explain their personal experience of gender balance, why it worked and what was good about it. When leaders script personal stories and tell them often, they bring a clear, simple and compelling focus to the topic and create an emotional connection. In a masculine culture, people are not going to change because there's a rule for it; they'll change when there are new expectations from people like them in leadership roles.

Another CEO in one of the Male Champions of Change groups says it has been a good opportunity for inquiry and curiosity. He admits that he doesn't get it fully himself. That's fine, because what he does get is how important it is to his business's future. That's a growth mindset at work. It's not about doing something for the sake of it or to look good; it's about finding meaning and purpose, and understanding why this has value to the organisation.

The leadership action that is required is to emphasise a more constructive style of leading. This direction and clarity will help organisations attract and retain more diverse workforces, which in turn will yield them the diversity bonus.[4] It is a leadership role to clarify what is acceptable behaviour. When that reset is focused on achieving a balanced culture, diverse people will be attracted and retained in the organisation. Figure 9.2 shows the relationship between leadership, culture and attraction of diverse talent.

Clear leadership responsibility reduces the tolerance of narrow, stereotyped behaviours. It makes it possible to both attract and keep a diverse workforce.

Leadership drives culture, which in turn drives attraction and retention of diversity.

It's going to take time for women to move into engineering and trades roles, for example, and for them to move up the ladder. BHP has targeted 50:50 representation. Others are following. Companies that want to stay competitive for the best talent will need to be equally attractive to women and men, as well as to minorities.[5]

Figure 9.2: How leadership affects culture and the attraction of diversity

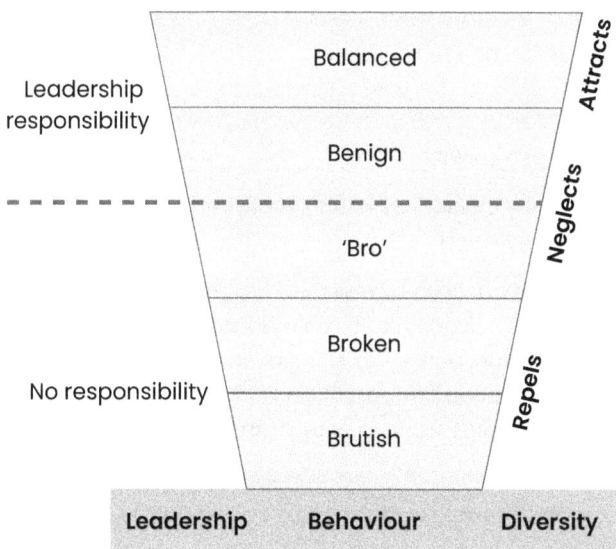

Clarity about what to do promotes action

If it isn't clear, it won't be done. Organisations need to make sure that their initiatives and approaches to creating gender balance are clear.

What is a gender-balanced culture? What does it look like and how is it different from the existing culture? Being clear about what must change to get there is important. Leaders need to understand the gender dynamics of their culture. They need to call out imbalance and identify actions to achieve gender balance; collect and use data, such as engagement survey results and exit interview feedback; and pinpoint where action will be most valuable. This becomes the roadmap that shows which route to take, what kind of terrain will be traversed and what tools are needed in the kitbag.

+ A work in progress

HASSELL's strategy included 16 clear initiatives, which have since been regularly reviewed.

A key initiative was to promote 'all roles flex', to demonstrate HASSELL's genuine openness to flexible working hours. Their flexible working hours policy has since been updated to be more educative around flexibility. It's a work in progress. Leaders actively discuss flexible working hours with their teams.

A change in tone for 'Out of office' messaging that states that HASSELL supports flexible working has received positive internal feedback.

Balanced gender representation on interview panels has been achieved in Australia and is being implemented in offices in other locations. New recruits in Australia have commented positively on the process, adding that the organisation 'walks the talk'.

50:50 participation in HASSELL's 'Next Gen Conferences' has been achieved.

Initiatives that focus on promoting gender balance to the external world include gender balance in submissions for projects. According to Ingrid, HASSELL is managing this 'pretty well'. Given that they don't yet have balance at the senior levels, this target will take time to consistently achieve across the business.

They have achieved 50:50 attendees where they sponsor tables at events with clients. Their external communications promote women at all levels.

Coaching cascades strategy into everyday behaviour

It's in everyday 'normal' behaviour that culture comes to life. This makes coaching the go-to tactic for supporting a gender-inclusive culture. If leaders coach, they can help to moderate and manage the behaviour of team members to be constructive and inclusive.

The evidence shows that a masculine contest culture reduces safety, trust, learning and innovation.[6] There are diminishing returns for everyone if people are seen as expendable and not treated with care and respect. No-one wins the long game.

Culture and engagement surveys show that there is still too much competition and not enough care in many organisations.[7] The type of work is no excuse.

Research by Robin Ely and Debra Meyerson on offshore oil rigs (which you might think are as tough and manly as can be) shows how pliable culture can be when managed well. The researchers discovered a couple of rig teams that were achieving outstanding performance results and found that the teams were operating very differently to typical rigs. The business had experienced heavy accident and injury rates and management knew things had to change. Leaders set about creating a different culture to keep workers safe. They focused on the cultural expectations workers had about how they did their work; in particular, how they engaged with each other. Teams were inducted, retrained and set up with new expectations.[8]

The culture design focused workers on seeking to learn how to perform their jobs more safely. To do this, they needed to acknowledge physical limitations, learn from their mistakes and look after their own and others' emotions. They needed to engage in mutual expressions of vulnerability and to dial back on masculine behaviours.

The focus on learning and safety served to minimise competitive masculine behaviours. The oil rigs experienced an 84 per cent reduction in accident rate, as well as productivity, efficiency and reliability outputs that exceeded the industry's previous benchmarks.[9]

Key differences in the workers' behaviour were also identified. According to the workers' own reporting, rather than seek to prove their toughness, they readily acknowledged their physical limitations, publicly admitted mistakes and openly attended to others' feelings. As well, their relationships with each other were strengthened.

Even in an organisation comprised entirely of men, contest cultural norms have negative consequences. If oil rigs can achieve un-gendered behaviour even when there are no women present, pretty much any organisation ought to be able to do the same.

A culture that is gender-balanced in its approach, even if there are no women present, operates more effectively. The 'contest', if there is any, should be between what helps effective and safe work and what interferes with it.

It's all about gender, but it's not about gender at all

It is all about how the best leaders can be developed and supported to grow engaged and motivated workers who work well together.

Chapter 4 outlined a framework for inclusive leadership, and core to inclusive leadership is a coaching mindset. What is missing is that many leaders don't know how to be inclusive, and that's partly because they don't know how to coach. It's not necessarily the will that's lacking but the skill to do so. It's how leaders engage with people, every day, that matters. They need to coach to create safe and inclusive workplaces. It's a positive style that moves people in the right direction.

We can't assume that good leading comes easily. It's more complicated than that! We need to invest in growing the coaching skills and capabilities of leaders so that they are well equipped for this work.

Senior organisational leaders, as well as People and Culture leaders, have a big role to play to support leaders. If you're a People and Culture leader, here are some of the things you can do:

- ► Help leaders understand the value of diversity.
- ► Show leaders how to set up psychological safety for everyone in the team (and there's more on this in Chapter 10).

- Reorient leaders away from having to prove their masculinity and towards more compelling goals.

- Help leaders to ask more questions rather than tell others what to do.

- Help leaders understand how norms and practices affect the culture, and highlight unproductive behaviours that get in the way of performance and results.

- Provide leaders with processes and tools to give and receive feedback.

- Show leaders the value of flexible styles of leading.

- Give leaders skill development opportunities so that they can lead their teams inclusively.

- Make it clear and easy to assess talent fairly.

- Give leaders the skills to have difficult conversations.

Leadership development programs should prime leaders to coach for inclusion. To do so means developing leaders' mindsets, their responsiveness to others and their ability to manage group dynamics, as shown in Figure 9.3.

At the level of the individual leader, mindset may need to be reset. That's because when leaders coach for inclusion, they start with their own mindset. In particular, they prime themselves for leading 'people who are not like me'. The key question to help the shift is: 'How do I think about my role for creating inclusion and belonging for people who are not like me as well as those who are?' Simple question, challenging reset.

Figure 9.3: A coaching model to cascade gender-balanced culture

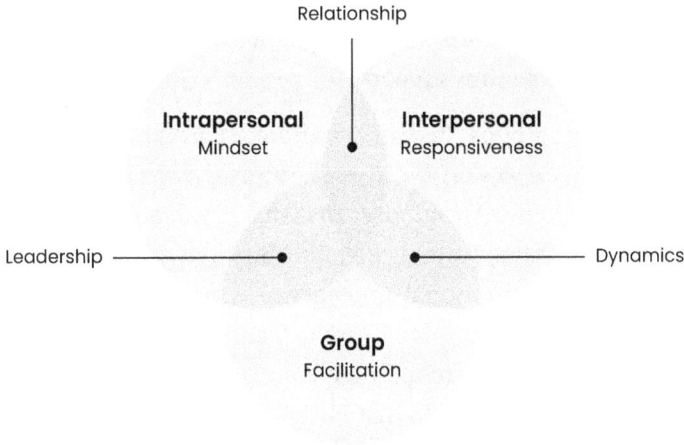

Relationship

Intrapersonal
Mindset

Interpersonal
Responsiveness

Leadership ——————— ———————— Dynamics

Group
Facilitation

Primed with that mindset, leaders then bring a relationship focus to their interactions with others and that means being responsive to their people and teams. They focus on building relationships across differences. The key questions to make the shift are: 'How am I responsive?', 'How do I take responsibility for establishing fair relationships with all my team members?' It's about working out how to work well together, not necessarily about liking others. In their relationships, inclusive leaders are responsive to make sure they are fair. That doesn't mean all relationships look the same; it does mean that everyone gets value.

We know that leaders spend more time with male team members, and more of that time focused on their career advancement, than they do with women. These are among the long-entrenched habits of leaders that need to be challenged.

Focusing on the team dynamics is a step up in challenge for leaders, and that's because many leaders do not have insight into the complexities of leading group dynamics. Working with different needs and perspectives is difficult, takes practice and requires support.

Facilitating groups to work well together and get good outcomes will always be a work in progress. Leaders who adopt a higher order mindset that this is valuable work will create more value from it. Relationships can seem complex, particularly if emotional intelligence is not high, which is when it becomes harder to shift the focus to team interactions and dynamics. In a group, there are many more people to be responsive to. How to do that fairly? The leader's focus turns to facilitating the interactions between others.

Ensure that dynamics are constructive, everyone's talents are included and the best outcome is achieved.

Chapters 10 to 12 provide more tools for leaders. There's more on how to set up positive working environments and manage the dynamics between team members.

Here are a few practical actions that leaders should be developing to include in their coaching repertoire:

Mindset
- Be humble and curious; ask first.
- Prime for relationship.
- Minimise your own need for power and status.

Responsiveness

► Take second position, seek to understand the particular experiences and needs of others.

► Ask for feedback and express humility and a willingness to learn.

► Delegate to show trust.

► Share tips for how to do things better.

Facilitation

► Manage equal turn-taking.

► Balance challenge and support.

► Minimise dominance, high power and status plays within the team.

Consistency encourages sustainability

To get more traction on diversity and inclusion in the future we need to peel back the culture onion from a gender point of view. We need to keep cycling between what is aspired to and espoused and what actually happens in the lived experiences that play out day to day. Diversity and inclusion need to be said *and* done. Keep measuring, so you can see your progress.

As what leaders say and do is core to culture, make sure you hold yourself and others to account. There's no point saying 'This is what our culture is', then letting transgressions go. Take a growth mindset and use bumps in the road as an opportunity to learn. (Part IV goes into more detail on this.)

+ To honour the culture, hold leaders to account

Laura (not her real name) is a senior leader in a global infrastructure company. She called me a couple of days after an interaction with one of her peers. She was feeling uncomfortable about the incident, and with her boss's response to it.

While they'd only been colleagues for a short while, Laura experienced her peer's behaviour as very masculine. He was argumentative. He needed to have the upper hand, he dominated conversations with all their peers and 'contested everything'.

The two had been negotiating about the temporary release of one of her people to his team. As they couldn't come to a mutual agreement, she'd asked the boss to arbitrate and make the decision based on overall business needs. The male colleague was clearly not happy with the decision, as it was not in his favour. He continued to approach Laura to tell her how this was inconveniencing him and to ask her to change her mind. Their HR consultant also did so, at the colleague's behest. Laura felt pressured and disrespected.

Then the behaviour escalated. He rang her, and over the phone shouted at her and abused her for not doing what he wanted. Laura felt shaken by the exchange. His behaviour was inappropriate. He had breached behavioural guidelines set out by the organisation.

Laura reported the incident to her boss, whose response was not as she expected. Firstly, she learned that her peer had already informed HR that there might be a complaint, which to Laura seemed like a pre-emptive move to absolve him of responsibility for his behaviour. Because her colleague had experienced a personal crisis seen as precipitating his behaviour, the boss put it back to her: did she want 'to take any action'?

What seemed unacceptable to me was that responsibility for the next action, the consequence of the peer's behaviour, was left with Laura. Organisational standards had been breached by a senior leader. There was no doubt about it. HR knew but didn't take any action, and the boss knew and left it to Laura to decide whether to take action.

The clarifying coaching question was: 'What would you do as leader if this had happened to one of your team members?' Laura was very clear about the appropriate leadership course of action. Whatever the personal circumstances surrounding her colleague, his behaviour had not been acceptable and he needed to be called out for it. The nature of the calling out and the consequences for calling it out might perhaps be moderated by his personal circumstances. Calling it out shouldn't have been in question.

Laura relayed her conclusions back to her boss, who was happy to proceed with appropriate action. This was a case of her boss needing upward coaching. Yet, it shouldn't have been left to Laura to decide what to do – the organisation's culture code made it clear.

When behaviours breach organisational standards yet action is not taken, masculine dominance behaviours continue. Women like Laura shouldn't have to feel this burden of responsibility for calling out inappropriate behaviour.

Examining the culture of an organisation is vital for increased balance and flexibility. There needs to be a work environment that supports psychological safety. Then men can re-examine how they contribute, expected behaviours can be articulated clearly and unhelpful behaviours can be called out.[10] And that kind of change is possible in even the toughest of environments, as the oil rigs research shows.

To maintain a consistent focus, diversity and inclusion must be kept on the agenda. Make sure they are always a part of the strategy and culture work of the organisation. Both Nick's and Ingrid's stories show that change happens over years, not months. Keeping it on the agenda helps sustain progress.

And keep the work focused on the willing. Whether or not they support diversity, men may feel threatened – either because they're being put in the spotlight, or for not knowing what they don't know. That's pretty challenging. Incidentally, some women may feel threatened too.

Minimise the threat by focusing on inclusion. Keep the focus on what's positive, what's workable. And don't leave out the fence-sitters.

Back in Chapter 1, the focus was on Champions and building a pipeline of Champions. Make sure you celebrate, support and make more Champions. Likewise, make sure you ignore Resistors. Champions make up the top 20 per cent of the pool and Resistors the bottom 20 per cent. That's 40 per cent of the people pie. In the middle, the remaining 60 per cent are watching and waiting to figure out what to do. This 60 per cent are what Susan Lucia Annunzio calls the 'movable middle'.[11]

It's by being consistent and consistently positive that the 'movable middle', well, moves. When they know what to do, and when it is safe to do it, the middle will also move to embrace gender balance.

Focusing on the middle creates more value than focusing on Resistors. It starts to move the majority of people to behave and support gender-balanced culture, and when the context changes, attitudes and beliefs also change. When the movable middle is on board, you've got culture change.

Changing gender-related habits might seem big, so break down what needs to be done into tiny habits and behaviours that make it palatable and doable.

Telling and repeating simple, consistent stories reinforces the power of change. James Clear in *Atomic Habits* shows how steadfastly focusing on one simple thing to change, and doing it every day, gives you a compound return. A 1 per cent change per day gives you a 37 per cent compound change in a year. That's better than trying to change by 37 per cent and only doing it for one day. Pick one thing that you can change, and repeat it until you have mastered it.[12]

Make it clear, keep it small, repeat it, and make culture change doable.

You can shape organisational leaders in the challenging task of culture change by pursuing one small adaptive action each day. If you have leaders who are keen or open but don't quite know what to do or how to do it, make them a priority. Give them one tool that they can practise each day, get feedback, practise some more, then try the next.

Bias Buster 9

Commit to an inclusive culture

To reduce the degree of contest in your culture, keep four things in focus:

1. Ensure clear, committed leadership messages.

2. Consciously assess and act in favour of a gender-neutral culture.

3. Provide more support for leaders so that they know how to be inclusive and do leadership well.

4. Provide leaders with encouragement, development opportunities and the tools they need. Then they can make change and progress, day to day.

PART IV

Walking the culture talk

We are what we repeatedly do.
Excellence, then, is not an act, but a habit.

— ARISTOTLE, SUMMED UP BY PHILOSOPHER WILL DURANT

Conversations about gender and difference can be contentious. Most of us mean well, but that doesn't guarantee that we have the conversations we need to have or that the conversations go as we would like them to go.

We can make more rapid progress on gender inclusion if we make progress easier to make. This section of the book is a guide to rising above 'political correctness'. It will help you navigate through the minefields and missteps of contentious conversations and provides tactics designed to clear the minefields. Its goal is to help you make conversations about difference easier to have and more meaningful in their impact. Your conversations will be authentic, less biased and more inclusive. Rise above the noise of 'political correctness' to stay authentic in your quest for greater inclusion.

It can be tricky to negotiate the differences between people. You need to understand other perspectives and be inclusive. We all have blindspots and don't even know what it is we miss or mistake. If we engage with the intention of being more inclusive, take a growth mindset and talk about it rather than avoid it, there are huge benefits to be had.

Not talking about it doesn't help and doesn't make it go away. Talking about it defuses it, creates new norms and helps us to beat our own biases. We are more likely to work together in an environment where people feel they belong and are respected for their individuality. When we meet these fundamental human needs, workplaces thrive and people prosper.

When we don't talk about our differences, we waste opportunity, misunderstand and stereotype others, and deny their experiences. We create distance and conflict. We maintain stasis. On the other hand, when we do talk about it, we make opportunity, understand and individualise. That defuses tension. We connect and unite across difference, and as a consequence we make progress.

We need to give up the need to have perfect conversations, the idea that *this* conversation is going to be the one that will fix everything. Instead, use your motivation to improve gender inclusion to increase the *number of positive conversations you have*. It will help avoid backsliding and stagnation. You will make more rapid progress.

The chapters in this section are a roadmap for better conversations. They're based on a 3×3 matrix (shown over the page) that matches the three levels of complexity in a conversation – the set-up, the pinch and the crunch – with the different kinds of tactics to use; 'what to do', 'who to be' and 'how to say it'.

- ► Chapter 10 details the set-up for constructive conversations. It's about getting the right context.

- ► Chapter 11, 'Pinch points', focuses on the niggling feeling we get when we know something's not quite right but we're not quite sure what. It focuses on how our brains trap our thinking and limit what we say, and it offers advice on how to notice a pinch and what to do about it.

- ► Chapter 12, 'The crunch', refers to the most complex kind of conversation, when the stakes and emotions are high. It offers suggestions about how to make the tougher conversations easier to have.

A roadmap to positive conversations

	The Set-up	**The Pinch**	**The Crunch**
What to do	1 Set the context	4 Notice the new	7 Sustain the focus
Who to be	2 Be better	5 Be an ally	8 Be a Champion
How to say it	3 Nip it in the bud	6 Call it out	9 Stop it

Tactics *(What to do / Who to be / How to say it)*

Conversation complexity

10

The set-up

We feel like we're walking on eggshells when we have conversations about gender. We're not sure what we should say, we're worried about saying the wrong thing, we don't want to offend the women in the room.

— HR EXECUTIVE

I'll never forget the conversation I had with the head of human resources at a large retailer. We were reviewing the agenda for a gender diversity workshop with the organisation's leadership team. He shared the concern in the quotation above, which he and some of his male colleagues had discussed among themselves.

The irony of the eggshell metaphor is that women in male-dominated work contexts often feel that they too are walking on eggshells.

I'm grateful that the HR executive was comfortable to share this concern with me. The conversation has been a marker for me ever since. It reinforces my view that it isn't that people don't want to have the conversation, or that men don't want to be part of it; it's just not clear enough *how* to take part.

None of us should feel like we're walking on eggshells.

When I work with leaders, I want to make sure that the scene is set for conversations that are safe; to avoid people feeling like they are walking on eggshells. I focus on how to have more positive, constructive and future-focused conversations.

Motivation to change is fuelled by a sense of progress. Make sure you don't backslide or stagnate. Increase your progress by increasing the number of positive conversations.

Figure 10.1: How positive conversations harness motivation for change

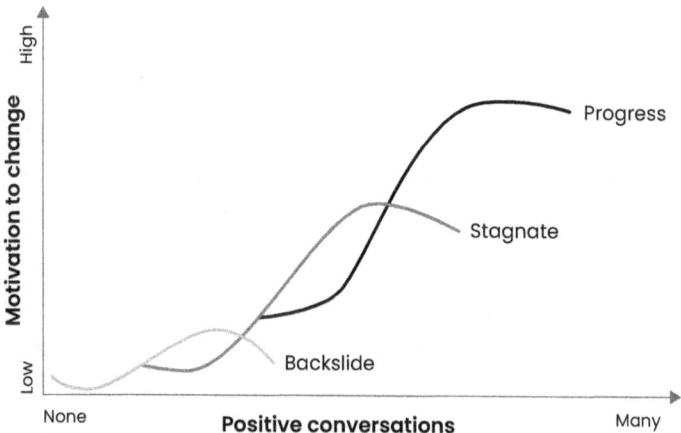

Set the context

What we need to do first is to set the context. Here's how to set up and what to do to get the context right for constructive conversations. Context counts. To make contentious conversations easier, I set an explicit context for them. I focus on three principles: curiosity, candour and confidentiality. They make a big difference to how people engage in the conversations.

In particular, they affect how much vulnerability people will show. Vulnerability is a prerequisite for talking about our beliefs with others, particularly when we are discussing our potential decision biases. Talking frankly about how our decisions might affect others takes courage and openness.

So how do I work to get that vulnerability? I do it by focusing explicitly on generating a safe foundation via the three principles that make up the context for contentious conversations. (See Figure 10.2.)

Figure 10.2: Foundation commitments for constructive conversations

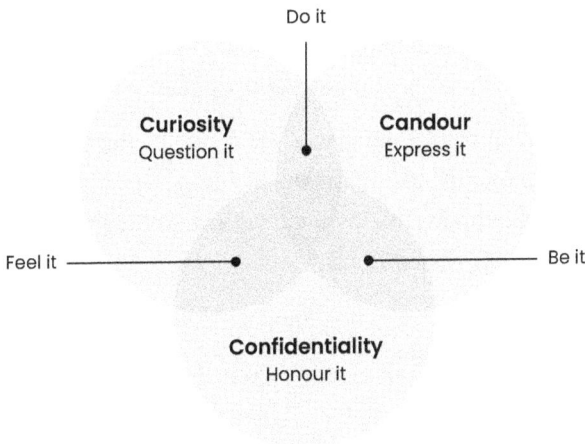

Do it

Curiosity
Question it

Candour
Express it

Feel it ——————●   ●—————— Be it

Confidentiality
Honour it

Curiosity

Even in small doses, curiosity gives us a burst of dopamine. This helps to make an experience feel rewarding. Stereotypes, gender imbalance and unconscious bias are all intriguing topics. They're a bit mysterious; we don't fully understand how they work. So we need to ask questions, to find out more, to explore what it's all about. Asking questions activates our curiosity.

That's a big plus for this kind of conversation because it reduces potential 'pain' and instead triggers enjoyment. When curiosity replaces contention, we increase the likelihood of future conversations on the same topic.

Candour

The eggshell metaphor comes into play here. All honest views need to be welcome, no matter what they are. They are only views.

The intention is not to inculcate a particular way of believing. Even if it was, it wouldn't work. When you suppress negative views they create a stronger effect. It's weird, but true! We don't want people to sit on their concerns or to avoid calling out inconsistencies. Get it out in the open, then discuss it.

It's important to say what you mean, to express your views with openness. It's as important to accept the right of others to hold and express their own views, even if they are different. Especially if they are different.

Confidentiality

Make being candid and curious about beliefs safe by emphasising confidentiality. Ask for agreement that all personal information shared in the conversation is confidential. The Chatham House Rule doesn't cut it here.

We want to be able to ask the 'dumb question', we want to be able to express divergent views, to disagree or to point out flaws. To do that we need to be sure that what we say is not going to be repeated and/or held against us.

This is hard to get right, because information is currency. Exchanging information gives us status. And we tend to diminish the rights of people whose views are different from ours. Setting the right tone here – by honouring confidentiality – is a powerful leadership act. Lay a strong foundation for great conversations: have participants commit to feel and be curious and candid, and to keep confidences.

Even very senior people need a safe context to engage freely in conversations about gender inclusion.

This was evident in a recent discussion with a leadership team comprised mostly of men. The relief from the men during the conversation was obvious. There were many questions and suggestions about what was happening and what to do. They didn't feel like they were walking on eggshells.

For some of the leaders, the focus and their questions were a little more personal. They sought to get a handle on the impact of their own behaviour. One felt shock that his actions contradicted his values and that he had been unaware that they did. It felt challenging for him and he wanted to better understand why this happened. Others were keen to explore what they could do to model inclusive behaviour. They felt satisfied to have had such a collaborative conversation.

Psychological safety is always important; more so in this area. With the right context, it's possible to name and discuss the concerns people have about gender inclusion. When the context isn't right, however, people's concerns can prevent further discussion.

Typical concerns include:

- fear of backlash
- actual backlash, including denial, rejection, inaction, placating, repression
- conflict
- relationship breakdown.

If you allay people's concerns, you will help significantly to increase understanding about gender, inclusion and leadership. Doing so will create a chance for people to explore actions for change and to inspire leaders to be more inclusive. And together you can create changes that improve leadership and working lives.

Normalising the challenges of these conversations works well for engaging others. It reduces the anxiety that 'difficult conversations' evoke for many of us. And it's also a way to 'be better'.

Be better

The next step on my roadmap is 'who to be'. The most effective actions to overcome bias come from those who care most about equality.

Recently, I was walking along an airport concourse and saw two pilots walking together. One was female and the other was male. There was a significant height difference between them. My immediate thought was, 'She can't be a pilot, she's not strong enough.'

Where did that come from? My tricky little unconscious associations, that's where!

I love it when there's a female pilot flying the plane! I love seeing women pursue careers in areas where they are under-represented. Unfortunately, this kind of mistake is easy to make. Like me, you may be one of the 75 per cent of people whose unconscious associations are stronger between male-and-career than between female-and-career.

Almost unbelievably (but as backed up by the research!), if you are a woman, then you are a little more likely to have these associations, and make these mistakes, than men are. Does it get more contentious than that?

Professor Dolly Chugh proposes a game-changing way to think about our identity when we act to increase inclusion. She makes a distinction that I find liberating. On the one hand, I could feel ashamed that I have such a thought about a female pilot. Or I could feel guilty because I did.

If I feel shame when I make this mistake, then I shut down the opportunity for my own growth. It's a threat to my identity to make sexist judgements about female pilots and I'd hide my mistakes from myself and others. Guilt, on the other hand, makes us ask ourselves, 'What happened there?' and then 'What can I do about that?' and 'What can I learn from my mistake?' We are more inclined to take the opportunity to be better next time.

Shame paralyses, while guilt catalyses.

What causes us to feel shame is that our beliefs about ourselves and our behaviour pivot around having an identity as a good person.[1] We see ourselves as good. We care that others see us as good. It's uncomfortable to think that I am making biased decisions about women. I am not sexist!

'Bounded ethicality' means that our ethical decisions operate similarly to unconscious bias; that is, our self-belief in our goodness means that we work very hard to protect our identity as a good person, we put a boundary around it that allows us to ignore our mistakes and missteps. Usually, we want to dissociate from our mistakes. This is where the notion of walking on eggshells comes from. We are too worried to make a comment, ask a question or take some kind of action in the conversation flow. We don't act when we could act. We do and say things we would not 'normally' say.

Our conscious incompetence kicks in. We are very uncomfortable with our own incompetence. Our energy is consumed by responding to the threat of being seen as not competent, not good; either by ourselves or by others. Part of the reason for this is because we think in binary terms: if we're not good, we're bad. Male or female. Right or wrong. Sexist or non-sexist. Feminist or not.

By seeing ourselves as 'good', we limit how much change we can make. When we see 'goodness' as something that is fixed, we're caught in the either/or trap. It's a fixed mindset that shuts down growth.

Figure 10.3: Fixed versus fluid mindset

Fixed   Flexible   Fluid

We can use the energy that comes from feeling guilt to switch our focus to being better, rather than being good. Then we open up the opportunity for learning and growth. We take action, and then call ourselves out if we got it wrong, or don't know whether we were right. If we take a growth mindset, we'll learn more.

Professor Chugh says it's a higher standard to be 'goodish', to focus on how to be better. We'll still make mistakes. But we will be more comfortable to notice them, and to call them out. Rather than something to feel shame about, we use mistakes to catalyse our learning and growth. We'll be less likely to keep making the same mistakes and we'll also show others that it's possible to engage in contentious conversations with a lighter touch. We will be more powerful as we do.

How to be better? Activate an inclusion growth mindset.

It might not be comfortable at first, especially for senior leaders, who are supposed to know what to do and how to do it. As Professor Chugh says in her 2018 TED Talk,[2] everywhere else we give ourselves room to grow. But not here. Yet it's here that it matters most, because these are the decisions we are making about our fellow humans.

When I share my pilot experience, I'm modelling that both women and men make these mistakes and that it's not about being perfect. It's about how important it is to be able to notice mistakes if they happen, learn from them and do better next time.

Nip it in the bud

To make it easier to have conversations across difference, nip contention in the bud. Conversations become more contentious when:

- We don't have them as soon as we first identify the need for them.

- We don't know how to have them and don't express ourselves very well.

- We don't get our message across and feel dissatisfied with ourselves and the situation.

- We begin to think negatively about the issue in question or the person we need to converse with.

- What's been unsaid for so long becomes an invisible weight and we feel stuck.

To nip contention in the bud, we need to commit to a safe context. Once that's in progress, we need to know how to have the conversations, so that we can engage in them sooner. We need some guidelines for what to say and how to say it, so that we can get our message across with respect. We need to have ways to shift our mindset from fixed and negative to positive growth. When our mindset is positive, we show up in conversations very differently. If we do these things, we prepare ourselves with the mindset and the skills to build common ground and avert some of the contention.

A powerful way to nip it in the bud is to share positive stories.

When leaders admit to their vulnerabilities and share what they've learned about working with gender differences, others will do the same. This is candour and curiosity in action. Stories show your commitment and your consistency, they show how to have an identity as an advocate for gender balance and they show others that it is worthwhile.

Stories help you to avoid the conversation killers of:

- facts
- superiority
- certainty
- aggression.

Stay away from facts and trying to change others' beliefs. People with differing views generally don't respond well to being told what to know or to believe. They already know, and already believe, just in different ways.

I mentioned in Chapter 9 the senior leader who was considered a sceptic. In my conversation with him, I asked him, from a place of curiosity, about his own experience of diversity. He shared a compelling story about working in a multidisciplinary team that had been brought together to run a challenging project. He talked about how it had been a wonderful experience, quite different from his previous experiences, and told me that he counted it as his best work experience.

He said that gender, cultural and functional role diversity gave the group a balanced, settled feel. Instead of trying to outdo each other, people were very open to listening to different ideas. Many more influences governed the solutions they chose. It felt multi-dimensional and it created a work climate different from any he'd experienced before.

I asked him to envisage such a working environment for his own business, which was very male-dominated. He didn't go back to his default position that it wasn't possible. Instead, he was able to connect with the inspiration of his story and envisage what it would be like if he had a more balanced workforce.

About a year further down the track, the CEO was delighted to report to me that this senior leader had become a strong advocate for gender inclusion. The shift came from a simple story about his own experience that he then shared with others.

Simple, consistent stories from high-status figures help to start new norms. Behavioural economists see this as a tool for powerful change. What we talk about and how we talk about it set the norms for our conversations. We may not notice the current norms, but they're there. We have a choice: we can stick with the old norms or we can create new, better norms.[3]

Conversation starters

Here are further tips for nipping it in the bud – key conversational tactics for influencing others:

► **Extend trust first.** I began the conversation with the senior leader above by asking him about his experience. I reinforced that he was the expert on his own experience and on what worked for his business. I didn't seek to change his mind or to give him facts; I simply sought to understand. I wanted us to have a real conversation in which he said what he believed rather than what he thought I wanted to hear. I needed his trust to do that. To start, I extended my trust to him.

► **Seek common ground.** Start with what you agree on before you discuss how you disagree. This increases trust and empathy.[4] Find out what motivates those around you. What's their own experience of difference? What's their interest in inclusion? Find common ground through shared experiences and motivations.

Begin with a positive experience; this reduces the perception of the size and importance of the area/s of disagreement. It makes the discussion about these areas easier.

► **Ask questions.** More curiosity! As well as humility! You don't need to know all the answers. By asking open questions and listening actively to the answers, you will increase your chances of identifying new options and mutually acceptable views. It's another way to shift the balance to the positive. For example, 'I am not sure what I don't understand. I'd like to know how you saw it.'

► **Listen to all views.** This is simple respect. It's also a way to surface new options and possibilities. Differences can divide. If we start to line up as male against female, then conversations become more difficult. Instead, if we listen to everyone's views, we start to hear everyone's individuality and break down the subgroups. That means we break the connection to stereotypes of male and female and open up more options for everyone.

You can even collect data about the time you spend listening. Note how long you listen to each person speak over the course of a particular meeting, or over a timeframe such as a week. Who is listened to, without interruptions, and who is interrupted? (You might make this public, or you might not.) Are all views being heard?

We need to hear first, then we can act on it. We can't act on everything and we don't have to agree with everything but we can listen to the ideas, perspectives and suggestions that everyone brings.

➤ **Validate different perspectives.** Regardless of whether you agree or disagree with others, thank them when they express their view. If people are going to continue to be candid, then they need to know it's safe to be so. Diversity isn't about everyone being the same. The more difference there is, the better.

Because of our biases, we notice some things and not others. We can't prioritise what we don't notice. We don't necessarily see or seek relevant information, because we take our own perspective into conversations. Listening to different perspectives helps to increase what we notice and it gives us the option to adjust our priorities in response.

Bias Buster 10

Get set up for positive conversations

- Make it psychologically safe to be in your team; ensure the commitments are clear and consistent.

- Encourage a growth mindset and model it.

- Create your story about why this is important.

11

Pinch points

The competitive edge you get when
you accept diversity is worth the struggle
of getting there.

— GIAM SWIEGERS

Notice the new

When people experience a sense of progress, they are more intrinsically motivated.[1] The single most important factor in motivating people to put in effort is the perception that they are making meaningful progress. An optimistic, action-oriented focus creates forward momentum.

Progress on gender equality hasn't been easy, but it has been made. The progress you make in your own behaviour, team and organisation might not be as fast as you would like it to be. You can speed it up, and make it easier, if you notice the progress that *is* being made.

Organisational leaders set the tone when they notice and share progress. The amount of progress being made might seem small. The best way to use our effort to make progress is to remain aware of even very small signs of progress. Notice some signs every single day. Share your own. Share others' stories. Tell progress stories whenever you can.[2] This magnifies motivation to make progress.

A relentless focus on progress will speed the rate of change. We need to see the task ahead as drops of rain falling, collecting and being channelled along rocks. As it collects and gathers force, the runnels go deeper and wider. The flow increases and gathers power. The underlying rock is eroded and the runnel becomes a river that becomes a waterfall. Like water pouring over a waterfall, each drop, each surge of progress erodes the resistance, deepens the possibilities and increases the momentum.

The ability to notice even small amounts of progress reduces the impact of setbacks. It boosts positive emotions and engagement and it sustains effort to achieve long-term outcomes. Progress motivates people to accept difficult challenges more readily and to persist longer.[3] With attention focused on progress, we are again shifting the norm. Give up complaint and negativity; they sap energy. We can create a virtuous cycle instead of remaining in a vicious one.

Change will continue and endure if there is a positive sense of hope.

There needs to be a clear invitation for men and women to take positive actions that are inclusive, not divisive. That way, the momentum will continue.

Be an ally

Be brave and advocate for gender diversity. Step in as an ally when you get that niggling feeling that things might not be okay. Don't leave it to women or those affected by unfair or poor behaviour to do all the gender-inclusion work. Be an ally. Everyone can be an ally and advocate for gender inclusion, no matter their gender identity.

By being an ally, you reduce bias and you show other people that support counts. You show others that it's safe to speak up with concerns and questions about identity and opportunity. You make gender inclusion matter. You model your growth mindset and encourage others to grow too.

To magnify your contribution to change, deliver well-articulated and congruent messages about inclusion and your commitment to it. You don't have to have a senior role to play a meaningful part.

Small acts of advocacy are all it takes to make a social movement. As an ally, you help avoid the bystander effect. The more people there are to help out, the less likely it is that anyone will actually help.[4] If others don't notice bias, and you do, you can play a part to help others to notice it and to prevent it in the future.

Advocacy increases inclusion. You can increase inclusion by using your voice within your network. By speaking out more about the importance of gender inclusion, you can create more inclusion. More people will feel included and more people will join you as allies because they experience a greater sense of belonging.

Being an ally makes a difference, but we don't always feel comfortable with advocating. Some people don't advocate because they think that saying it once is enough – 'If I say it once, everyone will get it.' You'll see through that one straight away if you have kids or work with them! Adults aren't that different.

Another reason we don't advocate more is because others are advocating, and we think their efforts will be enough for the message to get through. 'It won't make any difference if *I* do.'

Still others don't advocate because they don't think their single voice has much weight; it doesn't seem worth it.

The harder thing that stops people advocating as allies is that they don't believe they can be powerful enough to make change. It seems to take a lot of effort without a guaranteed outcome.

I admit that for many years I didn't advocate as much as I wanted to or felt I should. I was concerned about being marginalised for being too vocal. It can be risky in certain contexts to be the lone female raising your voice and your visibility. Yet when I decided I would advocate more, I found that people around me were relieved and they joined in with my advocacy.

Advocacy that resonates with those around you is like a swarm of starlings, a murmuration. When the individual birds come together, they create a powerful and amazing sight. The magic of it is that this happens because each bird pays attention to seven of their neighbours. All it takes is for seven to pay attention to each other, to get in sync, and they create something extraordinary.

Just like the starlings, you don't have to advocate to all people all of the time. Your circle of concern might be the whole flock but your circle of influence is smaller than that. So don't over-extend; work your circle of influence. Focus on seven key people around you and influence them.

Figure 11.1: Focus on your circle of influence

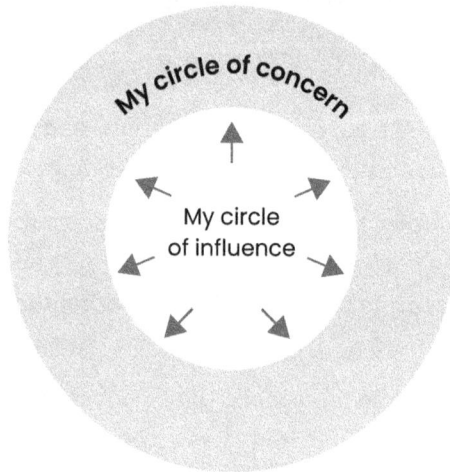

Advocacy starts with appreciating, and using, your own power.

Get clear about where you stand. What value does gender inclusion have to you? What will it mean to you when people are more tolerant and welcoming? What is a brief story you can tell that demonstrates the value you see?

Advocating for diversity has many benefits. When pro-diversity beliefs are expressed in a group, the group gets on better.[5] When people have pro-diversity beliefs, they believe that the differences between them bring a special value to the group. And a diverse group performs much better than a group of similar people. Believe in the value of a diverse group, and advocate that value to others, to improve the experience of working together.

If you can find alignment on important issues, strong messages about their importance cause our brains to click together.[6] When we get the 'click', we process information in the same way, 'with one mind', and we are more likely to share points of view. We are literally in sync with each other and this magnifies the shared motivation for change. If everyone in your circle is clicking, then they have the opportunity to do the same in their own circle, so that the clicking spreads.

Call it out

There are two ways to call out bias that I want to explore here. The first is your own potential for bias and how it may affect what you notice and what you do. By calling out your own bias, you make it easier for others to notice theirs. The second is the bias that occurs in conversations and how you can step in when you notice it.

Call out your own bias

There are six useful tactics that can help you call out your own bias.

1. Accept that you are not fair

The world isn't fair and we humans are not innately fair. Being an ally means firstly recognising this. Demographic differences mean that people are treated differently. If we believe that the world is fair, we reduce our awareness of how different people's experience of the world is and how differently they are treated. So, call it out when you notice it, question it and offer your support.

2. Notice your bias

If you can notice that different people are treated differently, then you can be more aware of your own bias. How much bias is activated depends on momentary changes in your attention.[7] You might perceive a frown by someone like you as an expression of thoughtfulness, yet when someone different from you does the same you perceive it as criticism. Noticing these micro-perceptions and small behaviours can be quite eye-opening. Our biases affect who we make eye contact with, and whether we smile or frown.

These behaviours are so small that they seem as if they ought to be inconsequential, but they are not. They build into what we say and how we say it, how long we spend with others, how much effort we put into understanding them, whether we promote them. People make judgements, and feel judged, based on these tiny cues.

In her book *The Loudest Duck*, leadership and diversity advocate Laura Liswood talks about the hyper-vigilance that minority group members feel.[8] If you're part of the elephant herd, you don't notice the mouse in the room but if you're the mouse in the room you certainly notice the elephants.

Collect some data on your own interactions. Who do you spend most time with? Who do you review your products and/or services with? Whose advice do you seek? Who do you not include in meetings? Take a growth mindset with you and get curious about your bias. Share with others what you are doing and what you find.

3. Check your privilege

There is a psychology of privilege that works like this:

We don't judge group disadvantage in the same way as personal disadvantage.

When confronted by group disadvantage, we tend to minimise the group's disadvantage and play up our own. We fear that others will see our privilege as unearned and in a sense we dissociate ourselves from it. For example, people who use family connections to get a job don't see that as advantage; they believe that they have won the job on merit. When they hear of others who used family connections to get a job, they see them as benefiting from advantage and judge them as less qualified.[9] The rules applied to others' behaviour are different from the rules we apply to our own.

If we reflect on the privilege that we hold as being part of a dominant group, such as men or whites, then we are less likely to minimise our advantage. For example, we can reflect and remind ourselves of our values (for example, fairness) or we can reflect on our personal successes.

Checking your privilege means reflecting on the ways that you may have relative advantage in your workplace. Metaphorically give yourself a pat on the back for what you have achieved, and it will be easier to see the disadvantage that others face. You might believe that others around you would also benefit from checking their privilege. Give them a pat on the back for what they have achieved. Then talk to them about group advantage and disadvantage. They will be more likely to appreciate their personal advantage and be more open to seeing the disadvantages that others face. If they can check their privilege, they are more likely to notice the disadvantage, and then they can act on it too.

4. Look for contradiction

Looking for contradiction is a great way to counteract the effects of confirmation bias. As discussed in Chapter 8, once an unconscious association activates we seek out information that confirms it, even if we don't know it is activated. We pay more attention to the information that supports it, while discounting what doesn't.

One example of this is how we judge women's confidence. The notion that women lack confidence is a strong meme. As we have seen, it is consistent with stereotypes of women as submissive, gentle and unsuited for senior leadership roles. If one woman in a group of women displays submissive and tentative behaviour, we are most likely to notice her – because she confirms what we believe about women's lack of confidence. In the process, we ignore the fact that the other women don't appear unconfident.

To counteract this, look for contradictory information about women and confidence.

One of the things we know is that women are penalised when they are too confident. When they are too confident we label them as aggressive, or 'more manly than the men'. We then dismiss their accomplishments. Keep a watch out for confirmation bias creeping into play!

5. Empathise with 'otherness'

The more power you have, the less likely you are to pay attention to others and their needs – your empathy diminishes. The higher up the ladder you are, in general, the less socially responsive you are. You tune in less to others and more to your status.[10]

If you have higher status that those around you, avoid jumping into conversations to assert your view. Let others have their say. Avoid disagreeing with those who have different perspectives. Dominate less. Switch from arguing for your perspective, and listen instead to the perspectives of others. Activate second position: 'How do you see this?' 'What is your experience?'

People in the dominant group can be blind to the idea that others experience the world differently; they see their own experiences as universal. Yet those who are different are constantly reminded of their 'otherness'.

Professor Dolly Chugh uses this example: in research on hiring patterns, white male managers who hired people just like them experienced no penalty in their performance ratings, while non-white male managers who hired people just like them did suffer a penalty. The non-white managers were assessed against a different standard.

'Other-ising' people can also be a consequence of good intentions. We put women on a pedestal, decide on their best interests, do good *for* them. This is just another way to treat them as 'other'. Check yourself – whose interests are being served? Yours, or theirs? Focus on empathy; tune in to them and their needs.

The more we interact with and get to know people, the less we 'other-ise' them. Look at your network and who you interact with. How might you increase its diversity?

6. Say it, ask it

Bearing in mind the commitments to safe conversations, one of the simplest ways to call bias out is to say what you think and to ask questions. Some of the options are: 'I don't know what to say', 'I'm not sure of how to respond', 'I feel out of my depth' or 'I really haven't noticed that before'.

Focus on a growth mindset and ask from the perspective of 'I don't understand X', 'I'd like to know more about Y', 'That didn't seem to go well – I'd like to know how I can do better next time', 'What am I not noticing here that's obvious to others?'

Follow-up questions are great. If someone makes a point, then ask a follow-up question. That allows people to feel validated, understood and listened to.

Call out conversational bias

There are three main pinch moments that many women experience in conversation: the 'speaking up' double bind, 'hepeating' and displays of dominance. Here's what they are and how to call them out.

The 'speaking up' double bind

The 'speaking up' double bind is something that most women have experienced. We tell women to speak up more, but when they do they're penalised for it. Males who speak up are seen as 10 per cent more competent than their peers while women who do the same are seen as 14 per cent less competent and are more likely to be labelled 'aggressive'. There's a real dilemma about whether to speak up.[11] Many women I coach have expressed their frustration at their experiences of the 'speaking up' double bind.

To call this out, you need to notice it. Pay attention to how much women contribute in meetings. Listen to attributions about their contribution. If you believe you are witnessing this double bind, here are three questions you can ask:

1. Are we sharing equal time? Let's check. Let's hear from everyone in the group.

2. When you notice attributions, go back to describe the actual behaviour. Encourage people to refer to behaviour and avoid judgements.

3. Challenge the differences in how we accept men's and women's contributions.

'Hepeating'

Even very successful women have the experience of having their ideas ignored or stolen. Minutes after a woman introduces a new idea that nobody seems to have noticed, a man repeats the same idea, winning the acclaim of those present. The phenomenon now has its own term: 'hepeating'. The term, a twist on 'repeating', was coined by a friend of astronomer Nicole Gugliucci. Naming the behaviour serves to make it more obvious and easier to call out.

If you notice that you are being given credit for someone else's idea, redirect the credit back to them.

Julie Bishop, while she was still Australia's Minister for Foreign Affairs, called it out when she declared that the days of allowing men to take credit for women's ideas were over.[12] You can help change this pattern by becoming a 'micro-sponsor'. A micro-sponsor shows how to respond when 'hepeating' occurs. When women's ideas are stolen, micro-sponsors call it out and give credit back to the idea's originator.

When micro-sponsors notice 'hepeating', they:

- Divert attention back to the person who generated the idea.

- Identify the person as the owner of the idea.

- Acknowledge the merits of the idea.

- Allow airtime to the originator to expand on the idea.

- Ask others for their views.

If 'hepeating' is familiar to you, name it and suggest a protocol for how to interact in meetings so that everyone's ideas are acknowledged.

- Give permission to call out the behaviour and say why you are.

- Include a no-interruption rule, so everyone gets a chance to pitch their ideas.

- Emphasise turn-taking and collaboration.

The greatest value of micro-sponsorship comes from the standard that team leaders set. If you are a team leader, what's your standard?

If you feel that your ideas are stolen, not noticed or not recognised, you can advocate for yourself. There are four ways you can call it out:

1. **Formulate your idea clearly.** In the conversational flow, ideas may not always be expressed clearly and may not be fully developed. Take the time to formulate and express your idea more clearly. Slow down your speaking rate. Summarise your idea, repeat it so that your audience has time to hear it. Make it a statement not a question.

2. **Claim your idea as your own.** I like the idea of bookending your idea with your claim to ownership. You can do this if you've thought through your idea before sharing it. For example, 'This is my idea. [Present your idea.] What do you think?' or 'I've been thinking through the way we approach x... [describe your approach]. That's my contribution to how we approach it.' Even if you don't start with a bookend, finish with one. Use 'I' and 'my'.

3. **Hold your audience's attention.** Show your enthusiasm for your idea and use that enthusiasm to create energy and hold attention. Also try these nonverbal tactics to go with your words: increase the volume of your voice slightly and use more expansive gestures. Examples of expansive nonverbal gestures include holding your chin up a little higher, opening your eyes a little wider, sitting taller in your chair, using hand and arm gestures that increase the space you take up, and leaning forward slightly.

4. **Ask for feedback on your idea.** Finish your idea by asking for feedback.

If you're interrupted partway through your idea, what can you do?

- Stay calm. Breathe.

- Take back attention. As soon as you can, revert to your unfinished idea. 'Let me finish that idea I started just a couple of minutes ago. [...]', 'I didn't quite get to the end of my idea to [...] I'll summarise my thinking [...] and let me finish with [...].'

- Try the 'broken record' technique. Repeat the idea... and repeat...

If, a few minutes later, someone else picks up your idea without acknowledging it, reclaim your idea. Start by thanking the person for picking up on your idea. Acknowledge any improvements they've made. Identify any omissions that you think are important. For example, 'Thanks Sam. I'm pleased that you've picked up on my idea to [...]. I like the [addition] you've suggested. I also liked my original point to [...]. I notice that you've left that out. It's important, because [...]. What does everyone think?'

Not paying attention to women's voices deprives organisations of valuable ideas. When women challenge the system and suggest new ideas, team leaders view them as less loyal and are more likely to discount their suggestions.[13]

All team members have their part to play in better managing conversations. Everyone can support the generation and recognition of ideas from all team members. And of most value are team leaders who get it. The greatest value comes from the standard that team leaders set. I encourage team leaders to better understand, attune to and manage the hidden dynamics of conversations that diminish women's voices.

Displays of dominance

The opposite kind of pinch moment is when there is a display of too much dominance. Dominance includes talking more often without giving others an opportunity, speaking at a higher volume and interrupting others. It includes over-using expansive gestures such as chin thrusting and vigorous hand gestures. These gestures all take up more space. When dominant individuals take up space for themselves, they crowd out others.

The antidote to over-dominance is collective intelligence, or a combination of average social sensitivity of group members, equality of conversational turn-taking in group discussion, and the number of women in the group. Women generally show greater social sensitivity and this is why gender-balanced teams often perform better.[14] Collective intelligence behaviours ensure that everyone has an opportunity to contribute their best ideas.

In summary, everyone in every conversation can make a contribution to reducing bias. Pay attention to the conversation dynamics, advocate for inclusive practices and call out practices that shut women down.

Bias Buster 11

Call out conversation pinch points

- Stay optimistic. Be positive. Keep emphasising the progress that is being made.

- Focus on your circle of influence.

- Work out the 'call it out' tactics that you are most comfortable using, then increase their use.

12

The crunch

The standard you walk by is the standard you accept.

**— DAVID HURLEY, FORMER CHIEF OF
THE AUSTRALIAN DEFENCE FORCE**

Sustain the focus

Make the focus on gender balance sustainable. Create a set of targets that you aspire to, and track them so that you notice their progress over time. Hold managers to account. It's not this year's fad, and it's not done when you finish writing the policy. Sustaining the focus and the energy means that conversations need to continue over time. A step in the right direction shouldn't stop another step. It takes an inclusive mindset to get the most out of the diversity in the room.

By sticking with it, you make it contagious to increase women's representation.

The BBC increased its representation of women in front of the camera by 74 per cent between 2017 and 2019. It began with the nightly *Outside Source* program anchored by Ros Atkins, which increased the number of on-air female contributors from 39 per cent to 50 per cent in just four months. By April 2019 there were 50 per cent or more female contributors on 74 per cent of the English-language shows.

Organisational behaviourist Aneeta Rattan and her colleagues investigated how this happened.[1] There was no diversity policy and a white man instigated the change. The starting point was daunting: in 2015, 19 per cent of front-of-camera experts and 37 per cent of reporters were female.

The researchers identified three key areas that they believed made the difference.

Firstly, decide to make change. You can opt in or opt out. Ros, the presenter, decided he would opt in. He aimed for 50:50 and then got on with it in his own area of control. He made the decision, then acted on it.

Secondly, make the change obvious. You need to collect data, because it's key to noticing change. Without the data you don't know what's going on, and without the data you won't notice the change you make. Make it easy, so embed data collection in a daily/regular routine. Ros's team decided what data they needed, they kept it simple and they collected it themselves. They then had control over it.

Finally, make change contagious, not compulsory. Because one team at the BBC was successful in making the change, it inspired others to see change as possible. Ros's team became a role model for other teams. Senior leaders opted in, then encouraged, rather than demanded, change. There was a growth mindset and no shaming or punishment for not opting in. It became desirable to be involved.

Before this, there had been efforts to increase gender diversity and inclusion at the BBC but none had been particularly successful. The example shows the impact of a sustained, committed approach. It started at the local level and then spread through other parts of the organisation. It was about the conversations one person decided to lead because he felt committed to gender balance. Daily conversations and the regular data collection kept them on track.

Be a Champion

As discussed in Chapter 1, the role of Champions in calling out gender bias, and stopping it, is critical.

It's important to add that being a Champion is not a personal PR campaign; with it come challenges.

A Champion doesn't do lip-service; words and actions need to align. Chapter 9 showed how to do that through leading cultural transformation for gender inclusion.

A Champion doesn't leave it up to others; Champions follow through. A Champion is vigilant and notices what people do. In particular, a Champion notices how leaders align their behaviour with the organisation's expected behaviours. There's clear guidance on how to be a good corporate citizen. When people don't do the right thing, or when they engage in the kind of behaviour experienced by our Asia Pacific CEO described in Chapter 2, Champions get straight on to it.

A Champion doesn't walk past it, no matter how small it is. If it's off-script, it's on notice.

Stop it

A senior leader in her organisation approaches Sarah. He is not her boss. He tells her that if she doesn't provide certain sexual favours then life is going to be very uncomfortable for her. She feels threatened, unsafe. She is concerned about her job and her career. She's also confused; she doesn't know what to do and she doesn't know who to turn to.

Focusing on what Sarah should do is important: she needs to feel safe and get support, then decide what to do. What happens next should be an organisational, not Sarah's, responsibility.

We need to shift the responsibility from women. Leaders need to make it stop.

Organisations are responsible for providing a safe context within which people like Sarah can do their best work. That is a key responsibility.

The news from the Australian Human Rights Commission (AHRC) on sexual harassment in the workforce is sobering. In 2018, in a sample of 10,000 workers, 23 per cent of women and 16 per cent of men reported being sexually harassed at work in the preceding 12 months.[2] Thirty-nine per cent of women and 26 per cent of men reported having been sexually harassed at work in the previous five years. People who identified as gay, lesbian, bisexual or of another sexual orientation were significantly more likely to be sexually harassed than those who identified as heterosexual: 55 per cent compared with 31 per cent. And of those who reported they had been sexually harassed, for 65 per cent it occurred more than once. Women were more likely to experience this than men: 69 per cent compared to 58 per cent.

Seventy-nine per cent of reported incidents were perpetrated by men, 21 per cent by women.

Only 17 per cent of those surveyed said they made a report or complaint – clearly people remain reluctant to report workplace sexual harassment formally. Over half of those who did report to their line manager made their complaint on the same day, and most complaints were dealt with promptly.

The harassment stopped for almost half of those who reported. About one third were praised for making the complaint. About 20 per cent received an apology from the organisation for failing to prevent the harassment. Forty-three per cent of those who reported sexual harassment experienced negative consequences. Some were labelled troublemakers; others were ostracised, victimised or ignored by colleagues. Twenty per cent of males and 5 per cent of females were disciplined and 17 per cent resigned.

Consequences for harassers included a formal warning (30 per cent), an informal warning (27 per cent) or the expectation of an apology (23 per cent). Twenty-two per cent were disciplined in some other way (22 per cent) and 12 per cent transferred to another work area. Nineteen per cent of those who reported said there were no consequences for the perpetrator.

A considerable challenge we face is knowing just what sexual harassment is. This is the legal definition provided in the AHRC report:

> *Sexual harassment is an unwelcome sexual advance, unwelcome request for sexual favours or other unwelcome conduct of a sexual nature which, in the circumstances, a reasonable person, aware of those circumstances, would anticipate the possibility that the person would feel offended, humiliated or intimidated.*[3]

The definition seems clear, but behaviour, and our response to it is much more ambiguous and varied than that. I may feel uncomfortable with behaviour that you don't even notice. So I might say, 'Stop it', but you don't. Or I might want to stop it but don't feel I can. We need to accept this degree of variation. We cannot let the variation distract us and we cannot justify inaction because of the variation. We need to act *despite* the variation.

As I said earlier, organisations say they are paying more attention to the prevention of harassment and management of claims and there has been an amplification by organisations of the term 'zero tolerance'. As *Financial Review* journalist Catherine Fox points out, deciding how to back this up is tricky and it relies on a legislative framework that does not yet exist.[4] The low level of reporting shows that there is still a way to go.

As I said earlier, organisations are responsible for providing a safe context within which people such as Sarah can do her best work. That is a key responsibility of organisations, yet it's not happening for her.

One way to increase the safety is to provide good sexual harassment training, and there are particular requirements to make sure sexual harassment training works. It's a touchy subject that's hard to do well.

The sexual harassment training paradox

Organisational behaviourist Dr Shannon Rawski found 25 per cent of participants of sexual harassment training experienced a negative reaction to it.[5] The training took a compliance focus, which is standard training for many organisations. (Remember the discussion in Chapter 3 that training backfired.)

The backlash against the training happened because this 25 per cent felt devalued, disrespected and deeply threatened. They felt like they were either harassers or victims themselves.

As a consequence, they:

- learned less than others about policies and practices
- didn't share information
- distanced themselves from potential victims
- increased their sex-based hostility and harassment.

This latter outcome is particularly concerning because some training may produce the very behaviours that we want to stop. So how does sexual harassment remain entrenched when we all condemn it?

Training can backfire and increase rather than decrease sexual harassment.

At a time of unprecedented action to prevent violence against women, and of increased acceptance of women in non-traditional work, the backlash comes as shocking news. If training doesn't work, we need to improve it so that it does. To prevent sexism, harassment and other forms violence towards women, organisational leaders and law enforcement agencies need to respond effectively when it occurs. Alarmingly, the 2018 review of the Victorian police service found that it had an 'entrenched culture of sexual harassment and discrimination'.[6] That is being addressed. Research like Rawski's is vital to help ensure the very agencies we rely on to protect us don't increase harm instead.

Understanding the process of backlash provides some insight into what's going on.[7] People are motivated to maintain self-esteem and their sense of identity in social interactions, and cultural stereotypes, including gender beliefs, are a critical part of identity. Initiatives that support women becoming senior leaders, or working in non-traditional areas such as policing, challenge our sense of identity. They promote behaviour that deviates from stereotypes, which in turn disrupts our expectations, causing an 'expectancy violation'.

Figure 12.2: How backlash occurs

Women understand that backlash is a possibility if they behave outside of gender prescriptions. Fear of backlash does two things.

Firstly, women stay within gender prescriptions because the backlash has disapproved of behaviour that deviates from those prescriptions. We saw in Chapter 3 that even very senior women used flirting in their interactions at the top leadership table.

Secondly, if they do behave in ways that violate gender prescriptions, women then engage in recovery strategies, including hiding or minimising their 'gender deviance'. They may lie about their behaviour, hide it or engage in particularly stereotypical behaviours to win back approval. Recovery strategies serve to reinforce stereotypes as well as enable people to maintain their sense of belonging to the group. They maintain self-esteem.

We saw in Chapter 3 that if people who are high in Social Dominance Orientation witness acts that violate stereotypes, they feel justified in taking punitive action. For example, people can believe it is within their rights to 'put women in their place', including when they are evaluating others in hiring decisions or performance ratings. Their self-esteem improves when they do. They feel better about themselves when they apply penalties for gender-deviant behaviour.

The fear of backlash applies to men as well as women and it also prevents men from appearing more 'feminine'.

Penalties apply to men who engage in stereotype-deviant behaviour. Research has shown that when men believe they are seen as more feminine, a common recovery strategy is to show stronger support for and engagement in physical violence, from wars to domestic violence.[8]

We also saw in Chapter 3, that for some men, having power over a woman appears to increase the likelihood of unwanted sexual attention. Women who display more assertion, dominance and independence experience the most sexual harassment.[9] And women who work in male-dominated organisations are harassed more than women who work in female-dominated organisations. The basis for the harassment is a hostility to the violation of gender ideals, rather than sexual attraction. This may explain why there is increased sexual harassment within the police and defence forces than in the general population. Victorian female police officers report more sexual harassment than women in the general public.[10]

What to do about backlash

There are many things leaders can do to guard against backlash from sexual harassment training:

- Be aware that backlash is likely, and stay attuned to its signs.
- Be aware that backlash comes from both women and men.
- Use inquiry and discussion to help improve the overall climate and work practices for everyone.
- Raise awareness of how unconscious beliefs and biases work.
- Ensure zero tolerance for harassment and discrimination.
- Hold people to account.

To make training work, change the nature of the conversation in the following ways:

- Give people a positive role to play in the training.
- Assume everyone is a potential ally, not a harasser or a victim.
- Recognise the elephant in the room – different people judge the same behaviour differently.
- Train people in empathy and conflict skills so that they can have difficult conversations about unwelcome behaviour.

Creating a safe work climate and ensuring that training focuses on caring for others are two crucial obligations for organisations. We need to talk about and do them.

Create a safe work climate

True safety cultures include psychological, emotional and sexual safety as well as physical safety. Organisations need to hold leaders accountable for the complete safety of their teams.

As a foundation, the work environment must be made safe for all workers. In addition, organisations need to pay particular attention to those who have lower levels of power. They need to ensure there is a zero-tolerance policy for harassment, and actively grow a culture founded on respect for others. Climate or engagement surveys can help to keep in touch with the level of safety people experience.

Leaders need to create a safe climate within their own team where people are encouraged and prepared to speak up. In addition, they ought to be paying attention to what's going on for their teams and among their peers. A peer calling out another peer on inappropriate behaviour is safety leadership.

The process for making an official complaint needs to be clear and have integrity. We already know it can be threatening for people who are being harassed to speak up about what's happening to them. Their reluctance to complain may be for fear of consequences, or because they don't know how to make a formal complaint. Our actions ought to be attuned to this and be prepared for it.

It helps to give voice to inappropriate behaviour in a safe climate that is reliable, one where people generally can speak up about what's happening around them.

Make training about caring for others

Sexual harassment should focus on taking care of your colleagues, and how to do that well. It's about noticing what is happening to others and having the confidence and tools to talk about what is going on. What do you notice, how do you say it, and how do you help to make it stop?

Having a known network of people or contacts to whom you can voice your concerns and have those taken seriously will also help. That way, there are open channels of communication focused on support.

Allies notice when someone is anxious or upset and they ask why. With allies around you, it's easier to speak up. It's much easier for someone who feels threatened and unsafe to reach out to an ally, someone who is more like themselves. Foster strong peer support networks so everyone has someone to go to if they need to.

Culture programs should make clear what good, respectful relationships look like. They can guide people on how to avoid 'crossing the line', what you should do if you think you have crossed the line, and what happens when you do. How can an organisation truly say it is committed to its culture if sexual harassment is occurring within it?

In the continuing absence of the right legislation to hear and resolve claims of sexual harassment at work, a focus on respectful relationships at work ought to be first priority. To create a culture that is true to their words, CEOs and boards must be both deeply committed to safety and advocate for equality. Nothing less is good enough.

Bias Buster 12

Use conversation crunches to stop bias

- Keep focused on the long game. Notice the incremental progress and build on it.

- Emphasise the value of Champions. Increase your own pool of Champions and promote what they do.

- Create a climate that doesn't tolerate harassment. Be clear that you don't and won't tolerate it. Step up if you have the slightest inkling it's occurring. Keep it on the agenda and make it about caring for others.

Afterword:
The future of leadership is inclusive

*As for the future, your task is not to foresee,
but to enable it.*

— ANTOINE DE SAINT-EXUPÉRY

As humans, we have traditionally related to people based on how similar or different they are to us. People are categorised as either 'like me' or 'other'. From an evolutionary perspective, this had advantages and kept us safe from harm. We now live in a very different world, one where our survival is no longer gained at the expense of others'. We live lives that are highly interconnected and the social boundaries and role ascriptions that served us in the past no longer serve us. Whereas homogenous groups used to serve us well, diverse groups are of primary importance to our future. This is exciting.

Tribes of the future will be global, cross-generational and cross-cultural and they'll be focused on innovation and growth, rather than on stasis and protection.

By replacing bias with inclusion, organisations will create personal and social value, as well as productivity and economic value, that will sustain future success – and they will do so in ways that are as yet unimaginable.

In this book, I have explained how biases, particularly of the insidious, unconscious kind, trip us up. I've outlined various approaches to take to minimise their impact. It might not be easy, and at times it is counter-intuitive, yet we can work to overcome them. Stereotypes are changing. When the context around you changes, the beliefs you hold change with it. The more inclusive we are, the easier it becomes to be inclusive. And in beating bias and increasing inclusion, my great hope is that we promote and support a much more positive focus for leadership, one that achieves results for the team and the organisation. The current masculine model is too focused on individual careers. We are blinded by confidence, narcissism and psychopathy.

Everyone wants to feel included and to make a difference. When organisations promote gender-inclusive leadership, that will be easier to achieve.

My Bias Busters are specific actions that you can take to outsmart bias, help advance the progress of women and create more inclusive cultures. I hope they make it easier for you to notice, talk about and overcome bias, create a climate of inclusion, foster a sense of belonging, acknowledge individual uniqueness and value people for their full talent. Support cultures that focus on safety, allow people to express themselves and appreciate the differences they bring.

Inclusive leadership promotes appreciation of different perspectives. When people feel a sense of belonging and that their uniqueness is recognised, they are more engaged. That is when the collective intelligence of the group to perform and innovate is more likely to be realised and the diversity dividend is more likely to be achieved. Organisations are more likely to be successful when they have high-performing teams that create innovative solutions to predict and respond to changes beyond our imagining.

This is the hard, and still undervalued, work of leadership. Leaders who promote inclusion avoid fault lines that fracture their teams. Inclusion helps level the playing field, and leadership promotes inclusive behaviour.

Let's look to the long game.

To encourage inclusive leadership, keep these four key things in focus:

1. By engaging people in the problem, let them control their own solutions to inequities.

2. Make sure your people are volunteers, and use curiosity as a key hook – this makes engagement rewarding.

3. Increase contact and connection between under-represented groups and ensure that they work together – this minimises status differences and focuses on work and learning.

4. Make responsibilities transparent and make people accountable for their actions – this will tap into their desire to look good to others.

I hope this book has opened up your thinking to the possibilities created by beating bias and being more inclusive. I hope that left-handers, women and other people in all our glorious individuality get to find their best place in the world.

There's a lot of work to do. And there are so many ways in which we can play a better part in a more inclusive world. Let's continue the quest for greater inclusion.

References

Part I

Chapter 1

1   Metz, I., *Male Champions of Gender Equity Change*. 2016, Melbourne: Melbourne Business School.
2   Rudman, L.A. and P. Glick, *The Social Psychology of Gender*. 2008, New York: The Guilford Press.
3   Male Champions of Change, *Our Experiences in Elevating the Representation of Women in Australia*. 2011, Australia: Australian Human Rights Commission.
    Male Champions of Change, *Our Progress Report*. 2017: Australia.
4   Male Champions of Change. *About Us*. 2019 [accessed 18 January 2019]; malechampionsofchange.com/champions.
5   Metz, I., *Male Champions of Gender Equity Change*. 2016, Melbourne: Melbourne Business School.
6   Smith, C.T., J. De Houwer, and B.A. Nosek, 'Consider the Source: Persuasion of Implicit Evaluation is Moderated by Source Credibility.' *Personality and Social Psychology Bulletin*, 2012. 39(2): pp. 193-205.
7   Morley, K.J., *Organisational Strategies to Counteract Bias*. 2018, www.karenmorley.com.au.
8   Fine, C., *Delusions of Gender*. 2010, Australia: Allen & Unwin.
9   Smith, C.T., J. De Houwer, and B.A. Nosek, 'Consider the Source: Persuasion of Implicit Evaluation is Moderated by Source Credibility.' *Personality and Social Psychology Bulletin*, 2012. 39(2): pp. 193-205.
10 Morley, K.J. *How to Inspire More Champions in Your Network*. 2019; www.karenmorley.com.au/inspire-more-champions-in-your-network.

Chapter 2

1   Chugh, D., *The Person You Mean to Be: How Good People Beat Bias*. 2018, New York: HarperBusiness.
2   Greenwald, A.G. and M.R. Banaji, *The Implicit Revolution: Reconceiving the Relation Between conscious and Unconscious*. American Psychological Association, 2017. 72(9): pp. 861-871.

3 Benson, B. *Cognitive Bias Cheat Sheet, Simplified*. 2017; Available from: medium.com/thinking-is-hard/4-conundrums-of-intelligence-2ab78d90740f.

4 Dasgupta, N., *Implicit Attitudes and Beliefs Adapt to Situations*. 2013. 47: pp. 233-279.

5 Kahneman, D., D. Lovallo and O. Siboney, 'Before You Make That Big Decision.' *Harvard Business Review*, 2011. June: pp. 51-60.

6 Kahneman, D., *Thinking, Fast and Slow*. 2011, USA: Penguin.

7 Morley, K.J., *Gender Balanced Leadership: An Executive Guide*. 2015, Melbourne.

8 Thiele, L.P., *The Heart of Judgment*. 2006, USA: Cambridge University Press.

9 Kahneman, D., *Thinking, Fast and Slow*. 2011, USA: Penguin.

10 Kahneman, D., D. Lovallo and O. Siboney, 'Before You Make That Big Decision.' *Harvard Business Review*, 2011. June: pp. 51-60.

11 Thiele, L.P., *The Heart of Judgment*. 2006, USA: Cambridge University Press.

12 Fine, C., *Delusions of Gender*. 2010, Australia: Allen & Unwin.

13 Rudman, L.A. and P. Glick, *The Social Psychology of Gender*. 2008, New York: The Guilford Press.

14 Ibid.

15 Morley, K.J., *Gender Balanced Leadership: An Executive Guide*. 2015, Melbourne.

16 Banaji, M.R. and A.G. Greenwald, *Blindspot: Hidden Biases of Good People*. 2013, New York: Delacorte Press.

17 von der Malsburg, T., T. Poppels, and R.P. Levy, 'Implicit Gender Bias in Linguistic Descriptions for Expected Events: The Cases of the 2016 United States and 2017 United Kingdom Elections.' *Psychological Science*, 2020. DOI: https://doi.org/10.1177/0956797619890619.

18 Berdahl, J.L., et al., 'Work as a Masculinity Contest.' *Journal of Social Issues*, 2018. 74(3): pp. 422-448.

19 Ibid.

20 Ely, R.J. and M. Kimmel, 'Thoughts on the Workplace as a Masculinity Contest.' *Journal of Social Issues*, 2018. 74(3): pp. 628-634.
Rawski, S.L. and A.L. Workman-Stark, 'Masculinity Contest Cultures in Policing Organizations and Recommendations for Training Interventions.' *Journal of Social Issues*, 2018. 74(3): pp. 607-627.

Edmondson, A.C., *The Fearless Organization: Creating Psychological Safety in the Workplace for Learning, Innovation, and Growth*. 2018, New Jersey: Wiley.

21 Morley, K.J., *Gender Balanced Leadership: An Executive Guide*. 2015, Melbourne.

22 Rawski, S.L. and A.L. Workman-Stark, 'Masculinity Contest Cultures in Policing Organizations and Recommendations for Training Interventions.' *Journal of Social Issues*, 2018. 74(3): pp. 607-627.

23 Ely, R.J. and M. Kimmel, 'Thoughts on the Workplace as a Masculinity Contest.' *Journal of Social Issues*, 2018. 74(3): pp. 628-634.

24 Berdahl, J.L., et al., 'Work as a Masculinity Contest.' *Journal of Social Issues*, 2018. 74(3): pp. 422-448.

25 Matos, K., O. O'Neill, and X. Lei, 'Toxic Leadership and the Masculinity Contest Culture: How "Win or Die" Cultures Breed Abusive Leadership.' *Journal of Social Issues*, 2018. 74(3): pp. 500-528.

26 Rawski, S.L. and A.L. Workman-Stark, 'Masculinity Contest Cultures in Policing Organizations and Recommendations for Training Interventions.' *Journal of Social Issues*, 2018. 74(3): pp. 607-627.

27 Ibid.

28 Eagly, A., M. Johannesen-Schmidt, and M.L. van Engen, 'Transformational, Transactional and Laissez-Faire Leadership Styles: A Meta-Analysis Comparing Women and Men.' *Psychological Bulletin*, 2003. 129(4): pp. 569-601.

29 Morley, K.J., *Gender Balanced Leadership: An Executive Guide*. 2015, Melbourne.

30 Hayne, K.A., *Royal Commission into Misconduct in the Banking, Superannuation and Financial Services Industry. Interim Report*. 2018, Australia: Commonwealth of Australia.

31 Ibid.

32 Rudman, L.A. and P. Glick, *The Social Psychology of Gender*. 2008, New York: The Guilford Press.

33 Matos, K., O. O'Neill, and X. Lei, 'Toxic Leadership and the Masculinity Contest Culture: How "Win or Die" Cultures Breed Abusive Leadership.' *Journal of Social Issues*, 2018. 74(3): pp. 500-528.

Chapter 3

1   Kray, L.J., et al., 'The Effects of Implicit Gender Role Theories on Gender System Justification: Fixed Beliefs Strengthen Masculinity to Preserve the Status Quo.' *Journal of Social Issues*, 2018. 74(3): pp. 98-115.

2   Matos, K., O. O'Neill, and X. Lei, 'Toxic Leadership and the Masculinity Contest Culture: How "Win or Die" Cultures Breed Abusive Leadership.' *Journal of Social Issues*, 2018. 74(3): pp. 500-528.

3   Glick, P., J.L. Berdahl and N.M. Alonso, 'Development and Validation of the Masculinity Contest Culture Scale.' *Journal of Social Issues*, 2018. 74(3): pp. 449-476.

4   Chamorro-Premuzic, T., *Why Do So Many Incompetent Men Become Leaders? (And How to Fix It)*. 2019, Boston, Massachusetts: Harvard Business Review Press.

5   Ibid.

6   Ibid.

7   Gillette. *We Believe: The Best Men Can Be*. 2019; Available from: www.youtube.com/watch?v=koPmuEyP3ao.

8   Leslie, L.M., 'Diversity Initiative Effectiveness: A Typological Theory of Unintended Consequences.' *Academy of Management Review*, 2019. 44(3): p. 538-563.

9   Dobbin, F. and A. Kalev, 'Why Diversity Programs Fail.' *Harvard Business Review*, 2016. July-August: pp. 52-60.

10 Ho, A.K., et al., 'The Nature of Social Dominance Orientation: Theorizing and Measuring Preferences for Intergroup Inequality Using the SDO7 Scale.' *Journal of Personality & Social Psychology*, 2015. 109(6).

11 Sidanius, J., et al., 'Social Dominance Orientation, Anti-Egalitarianism and the Political Psychology of Gender: An Extension and Cross-Cultural Replication.' *European Journal of Social Psychology*, 2000. 30: pp. 41-67.

12 Ho, A.K., et al., 'The Nature of Social Dominance Orientation: Theorizing and Measuring Preferences for Intergroup Inequality Using the SDO7 Scale.' *Journal of Personality & Social Psychology*, 2015. 109(6).

13 Kuchynka, S.L., et al., 'Zero-Sum Thinking and the Masculinity Contest: Perceived Intergroup Competition and Workplace Gender Bias.' *Journal of Social Issues*, 2018. 74(3): pp. 529-550.

14 Karp, P., 'Scott Morrison Wants Women to Rise but Not Solely at the Expense of Others.' *The Guardian*. 2019.

15 Ibid.
16 Jones, C.I., 'The Facts of Economic Growth,' in *Handbook of Macroeconomics*, J.B. Taylor and H. Uhlig, Editors. 2016, Elsevier.
17 Kuchynka, S.L., et al., 'Zero-Sum Thinking and the Masculinity Contest: Perceived Intergroup Competition and Workplace Gender Bias.' *Journal of Social Issues*, 2018. 74(3): pp. 529-550.
18 Rawski, S.L. and A.L. Workman-Stark, 'Masculinity Contest Cultures in Policing Organizations and Recommendations for Training Interventions.' *Journal of Social Issues*, 2018. 74(3): pp. 607-627.
19 Berdahl, J.L., 'The Sexual Harassment of Uppity Women.' *Journal of Applied Psychology*, 2007. 92(2): pp. 425-437.
20 Kray, L.J., et al., 'The Effects of Implicit Gender Role Theories on Gender System Justification: Fixed Beliefs Strengthen Masculinity to Preserve the Status Quo.' *Journal of Social Issues*, 2018. 74(3): pp. 98-115.
21 Munsch, C.L., et al., 'Everybody but Me: Pluralistic Ignorance and the Masculinity Contest.' *Journal of Social Issues*, 2018. 74(3): pp. 551-578.
22 Ibid.
23 Ely, R.J. and M. Kimmel, 'Thoughts on the Workplace as a Masculinity Contest.' *Journal of Social Issues*, 2018. 74(3): pp. 628-634.
24 Rawski, S.L. and A.L. Workman-Stark, 'Masculinity Contest Cultures in Policing Organizations and Recommendations for Training Interventions.' *Journal of Social Issues*, 2018. 74(3): pp. 607-627.
25 Dobbin, F. and A. Kalev, 'Why Diversity Programs Fail.' *Harvard Business Review*, 2016. July-August: pp. 52-60.
26 Ibid.
27 Rawski, S.L. and A.L. Workman-Stark, 'Masculinity Contest Cultures in Policing Organizations and Recommendations for Training Interventions.' *Journal of Social Issues*, 2018. 74(3): pp. 607-627.
28 Ibid.

Chapter 4

1 Chamorro-Premuzic, T., *Why Do So Many Incompetent Men Become Leaders? (And How to Fix It)*. 2019, Boston, Massachusetts: Harvard Business Review Press.

2   Cuddy, A.J.C., S.T. Fiske, and P. Glick, 'Warmth and Competence as Universal Dimensions of Social Perception: The Stereotype Content Model and the BIAS Map.' *Advances in Experimental Social Psychology*, 2008. 40: pp. 61-149.

3   Cuddy, A.J., M. Kohut, and J. Neffinger, 'Connect Then Lead.' *Harvard Business Review*, 2013. July-August.

4   Morley, K.J., *Lead Like a Coach: How to Get the Most Out of Any Team*. 2018, Melbourne: Major Street Publishing Pty Ltd.

5   Goleman, D., 'Leadership That Gets Results.' *Harvard Business Review*, 2000. March-April: pp. 78-90.

6   Chamorro-Premuzic, T., *Why Do So Many Incompetent Men Become Leaders? (And How to Fix It)*. 2019, Boston, Massachusetts: Harvard Business Review Press.

7   Ibid.

8   Morley, K.J. *How to Lead for Learning: It's Safety First*. 2019. www.karenmorley.com.au.

9   Homan, A.C., et al., 'Bridging Faultlines by Valuing Diversity: Diversity Beliefs, Information Elaboration, and Performance in Diverse Work Groups.' *Journal of Applied Psychology*, 2007. 92(5): pp. 1189-99.

10   Chamorro-Premuzic, T., *Why Do So Many Incompetent Men Become Leaders? (And How to Fix It)*. 2019, Boston, Massachusetts: Harvard Business Review Press.

11   Kuchynka, S.L., et al., 'Zero-Sum Thinking and the Masculinity Contest: Perceived Intergroup Competition and Workplace Gender Bias.' *Journal of Social Issues*, 2018. 74(3): pp. 529-550. Page, S.E., *The Diversity Bonus*. 2017, US: Princeton University Press.

Chapter 5

1   Page, S.E., *The Diversity Bonus*. 2017, US: Princeton University Press.

2   Ibid.

3   Jones, C.I., 'The Facts of Economic Growth,' in *Handbook of Macroeconomics*, J.B. Taylor and H. Uhlig, Editors. 2016, Elsevier.

4   Bersin, J. *Learning in the Flow of Work: Keynote Presentation*. 2018 [19 January 2019]; Available from: www.youtube.com/watch?v=niOI9VoS7IY&t=9s. CEIC. *What was Australia's Labour Productivity Growth in June 2018*. 2019 [18 January 2019]; Available from: www.ceicdata.com/en/indicator/australia/labour-productivity-growth.

5   Ahlback, K., et al. 'How to Create an Agile Organization.' *The McKinsey Quarterly*. 2017, McKinsey & Company.

6   Page, S.E., *The Diversity Bonus*. 2017, US: Princeton University Press.
7   Chugh, D., *The Person You Mean to Be: How Good People Beat Bias*. 2018, New York: HarperBusiness.
8   Eswaran, V. *The Business Case for Diversity in the Workplace is Now Overwhelming*. 2019 [4 January 2019]; Available from: www.weforum.org/agenda/2019/04/business-case-for-diversity-in-the-workplace.
9   Page, S.E., *The Diversity Bonus*. 2017, US: Princeton University Press.
10 van Knippenberg, D., 'Work Motivation and Performance: A Social Identity Perspective.' *Applied Psychology: An International Review*, 2000. 49(3): p. 357.
11 Coutu, D., 'Why Teams Don't Work.' *Harvard Business Review*, 2009. May: pp. 99-104.
12 van Knippenberg, D., C.K. De Dreu and A.C. Homan, Work Group Diversity and Group Performance: An Integrative Model and Research Agenda. *Journal of Applied Psychology*, 2004. 89(6): pp. 1008-22.
13 Homan, A., et al., 'Facing Differences with an Open Mind.' *Academy of Management Journal*, 2008. 51(6): pp. 1204-1222.
14 Bear, J.B. and A.W. Woolley, 'The Role of Gender in Team Collaboration and Performance.' *Interdisciplinary Science Reviews*, 2011. 36(2): pp. 146-153.
15 Page, S.E., *The Diversity Bonus*. 2017, US: Princeton University Press.
16 Ibid.
17 Ibid.
18 Ibid.
19 Ibid.
20 Ibid.
21 BHP. *Inclusion and Diversity: Partnering for Change*. 2020 [cited 30 January 2020]; Available from: www.bhp.com/our-approach/work-with-us/inclusion-and-diversity.
22 Pellegrino, G., S. D'Amato and A. Weisberg, *The Gender Dividend: Making the Business Case for Investing in Women*. 2011, Deloitte.
23 Dezső, C.L. and D.G. Ross, 'Does Female Representation in Top Management Improve Firm Performance? A Panel Data Investigation.' *Strategic Management Journal*, 2012. 33(9): pp. 1072-1089.
24 Woolley, A.W., et al., 'Evidence for a Collective Intelligence Factor in the Performance of Human Groups.' *Science*, 2010. 330: pp. 686-688.

25   Desvaux, G., S. Devillard-Hoellinger and M.C. Meaney, 'A Business
     Case for Women.' *The McKinsey Quarterly*, 2008. September,
     McKinsey & Company.
26   Pellegrino, G., S. D'Amato and A. Weisberg, *The Gender Dividend:
     Making the Business Case for Investing in Women*. 2011, Deloitte.
27   Adler, R., 'Women in the Executive Suite Correlate to High
     Performance.' *Harvard Business Review*, 2001. 79.
28   Page, S.E., *The Diversity Bonus*. 2017, US: Princeton University Press.

Part II

1   Banaji, M.R. and A.G. Greenwald, *Blindspot: Hidden Biases of Good
     People*. 2013, New York: Delacorte Press.

Chapter 6

1   Asgari, S., N. Dasgupta and N.G. Cote, 'When does Contact with
     Successful Ingroup Members Change Self-Stereotypes?
     A Longitudinal Study Comparing the Effect of Quantity vs. Quality
     of Contact with Successful Individuals.' *Social Psychology*, 2010.
     41(3): pp. 203-211.
2   Morley, K., *Why So Few Women in Science?* 2015: www.karenmorley.
     com.au.
     Logel, C., et al., 'Interacting with Sexist Men Triggers Social Identity
     Threat Among Female Engineers.' *Journal of Personality & Social
     Psychology*, 2009. 96(6): pp. 1089-1103.
3   Greenwald, A.G., et al., 'Understanding and Using the Implicit
     Association Test: III Meta-Analysis of Predictive Validity.' *Journal of
     Personality & Social Psychology*, 2009. 97(1): pp. 17-41.
4   Hilliard, L.J. and L.S. Liben, 'Differing Levels of Gender Salience in
     Preschool Classrooms.' *Child Development*, 2010. 81(6):
     pp. 1787-1798.
5   Stout, J.G., et al. 'STEMing the Tide: Using Ingroup Experts to
     Inoculate Women's Self-Concept in Science, Technology,
     Engineering, and Mathematics (STEM).' *Journal of Personality &
     Social Psychology*, 2010. DOI: 10.1037/a0021385.
6   Ibid.
7   Ibid.
8   Dasgupta, N. and J.G. Stout, 'Contemporary Discrimination in the
     Lab and Field.' *Journal of Social Issues*, 2012. 68(2): pp. 399-412.
9   *Beyond Graduation 2013*. Published in 2014 by Graduate Careers
     Melbourne.

10   Shumow, L. and J.A. Schmidt, 'Academic Grades and Motivation in High School Science: Associations with Teachers' Characteristics, Beliefs and Practices,' in *Handbook of Academic Performance*, R. Haumann and G. Zimmer, Editors. 2013, Nova Science Publishers, Inc.

11   Steffens, M.C., P. Jelenec and P. Noack, 'On the Leaky Math Pipeline: Comparing Implicit Math-Gender Stereotypes and Math Withdrawal in Female and Male Children and Adolescents.' *Journal of Educational Psychology*, 2010. 102(4): pp. 947-963.

12   Ebiquity, *Women In Innovation: Understanding Barriers to Innovation*. 2016, Innovate UK: UK.

13   Moss-Racusin, C.A., et al. *Science Faculty's Subtle Gender Biases Favor Male Students*. 2012.

14   Dasgupta, N. and J.G. Stout, 'Contemporary Discrimination in the Lab and Field. *Journal of Social Issues*, 2012. 68(2): pp. 399-412.

15   Ibid.

16   Ibid.

17   Ibid.

18   Fiske, S.T., N. Dasgupta and J.G. Stout, 'Girls and Women in Science, Technology, Engineering and Mathematics: STEMing the Tide and Broadening Participation in STEM Careers.' *Policy Insights from the Behavioral and Brain Sciences*, 2014. 1(1): pp. 21-29.

19   Dasgupta, N., 'Implicit Attitudes and Beliefs Adapt to Situations.' *Advances in Experimental Social Psychology*, 2013. 47: pp. 233-279.

20   Dasgupta, N. and S. Asgari, 'Seeing is Believing: Exposure to Counterstereotypic Women Leaders and Its Effect on the Malleability of Automatic Gender Stereotyping.' *Journal of Experimental Social Psychology*, 2004. 40(5): pp. 642-658.

21   Ibid.

22   Fine, C., *Delusions of Gender*. 2010, Australia: Allen & Unwin. Ibarra, H., R.J. Ely and D.M. Kolb, 'Women Rising: the Unseen Barriers. *Harvard Business Review*, 2013. September.

23   Rudman, L.A. and P. Glick, *The Social Psychology of Gender*. 2008, New York: The Guilford Press.

24   Eagly, A., et al., 'Gender Stereotypes Have Changed: A Cross-Temporal Meta-Analysis of U.S. Public Opinion Polls From 1946 to 2018.' *American Psychologist*, 2019. 18.

25   Banaji, M.R. and A.G. Greenwald, *Blindspot: Hidden Biases of Good People*. 2013, New York: Delacorte Press.

26 Heilman, M.E. and T.G. Okimoto, 'Why Are Women Penalized for Success at Male Tasks?: The Implied Communality Deficit.' *The Journal of Applied Psychology*, 2007. 92(1): pp. 81-92.

27 Mavin, S., 'Queen Bees, Wannabees, and Afraid to Bees: No More "Best Enemies" for Women in Management?' *British Journal of Management*, 2008. 29: pp. 75-84.

28 Sealy, R., 'Changing Perceptions of Meritocracy in Senior Women's Careers.' *Gender in Management: An International Journal*, 2010. 25: pp. 184-197.

29 Dezső, C.L., D.G. Ross and J. Uribe, 'Is There an Implicit Quota on Women in Top Management? A Large-Sample Statistical Analysis.' *Strategic Management Journal*, 2016. 37(1): pp. 98-115.

30 Asgari, S., N. Dasgupta and N.G. Cote, 'When does Contact with Successful Ingroup Members Change Self-Stereotypes? A Longitudinal Study Comparing the Effect of Quantity vs. Quality of Contact with Successful Individuals.' *Social Psychology*, 2010. 41(3): pp. 203-211.

31 Gratton, L., *Innovative Potential: Men and Women in Teams*. 2007, London Business School.
Krishnan, H.A. and D. Park, 'A Few Good Women – on Top Management Teams.' *Journal of Business Research*, 2005. 58: pp. 1712-1720.

32 Danaher, K. and N.R. Branscombe, 'Maintaining the System with Tokenism: Bolstering Individual Mobility Beliefs and Identification with a Discriminatory Organization.' *British Journal of Social Psychology*, 2010. 49(2): pp. 343-362.

33 Konrad, A.M., V. Kramer and S. Erkut, 'Critical Mass: The Impact of Three or More Women on Corporate Boards.' *Organizational Dynamics*, 2008. 37(2): pp. 145-164.

34 Homan, A.C., et al., 'Bridging Faultlines by Valuing Diversity: Diversity Beliefs, Information Elaboration, and Performance in Diverse Work Groups.' *Journal of Applied Psychology*, 2007. 92(5): pp. 1189-99.

35 Morley, K.J., *What Is the Best Way for Men to Champion Gender Equality?* 2017: www.karenmorley.com.au/best-way-men-champion-gender-equality.

36 Metz, I., *Male Champions of Gender Equity Change*. 2016, Melbourne: Melbourne Business School.

Chapter 7

1   Catalyst, *The Double-Bind Dilemma for Women in Leadership: Damned If You Do, Doomed If You Don't*. 2007, Catalyst: New York.

2   Borrello, E. *Professor Nalini Joshi, Mistaken for Wait Staff at Functions, Highlights Gender Bias in Australian Science*. 2016 [30 March 2016]; Available from: www.abc.net.au/news/2016-03-30/women-scientists-highlight-gender-bias-in-australian-stem/7285312.

3   Wertheim, S., 'The Common Habit that Undermines Organizations' Diversity Efforts,' in *Fast Company*. 2016.

4   Khadem, N., 'One of Asia's Most Powerful Women Used to Get Confused for the "Secretary",' in *The Sydney Morning Herald*. 2016.

5   Sandberg, S. and A.M. Grant, 'Madam C.E.O., Get Me a Coffee,' in *The New York Times*. 2015.

6   Malmström, M., J. Johansson and J. Wincent, 'Gender Stereotypes and Venture Support Decisions: How Governmental Venture Capitalists Socially Construct Entrepreneurs' Potential.' *Entrepreneurship Theory and Practice*, 2017.

7   Catalyst, *The Double-Bind Dilemma for Women in Leadership: Damned If You Do, Doomed If You Don't*. 2007, Catalyst: New York.

8   Ibid.

9   Davey, M.L., 'Women Start Out as Ambitious as Men, but it Erodes over time, says Researcher,' in *The Guardian*. 2015.

10 Williams, M.J. and L.Z. Tiedens, 'The Subtle Suspension of Backlash: A Meta-Analysis of Penalties for Women's Implicit and Explicit Dominance Behavior.' *Psychological Bulletin*, 2016. 142(2): pp. 165-97.

11 Heilman, M.E. and T.G. Okimoto, 'Why Are Women Penalized for Success at Male Tasks?: The Implied Communality Deficit.' *The Journal of Applied Psychology*, 2007. 92(1): pp. 81-92.

12 Unzueta, M., A.S. Gutierrez, and N. Ghavami, How Believing in Affirmative Action Quotas Affects White Women's Self-Image. *Journal of Experimential Social Psychology*, 2010. 46: pp. 120–126.

13 Crosby, F.J., et al., 'Affirmative Action: Psychological Data and the Policy Debates.' *American Psychologist*, 2003. 58(2): pp. 93-115.

14 Williams, M.J. and L.Z. Tiedens, 'The Subtle Suspension of Backlash: A Meta-Analysis of Penalties for Women's Implicit and Explicit Dominance Behavior.' *Psychological Bulletin*, 2016. 142(2): pp. 165-97.

15 Mayo, M., 'To Seem Confident Women Have to Be Seen as Warm.' *Harvard Business Review*, 2016. July.

16 Ely, R.J., H. Ibarra and D.M. Kolb, 'Taking Gender Into Account: Theory and Design for Women's Leadership Development

Programs.' *Academy of Management Learning & Education*, 2011. 10(3): pp. 474-493.

17 Ibid.

18 Jones, K. and E. King, 'Stop Protecting Women from Challenging Work.' *Harvard Business Review*, 2016. September.

19 O'Neil, D.A., M.M. Hopkins,and D. Bilimoria, 'A Framework for Developing Women Leaders: Applications to Executive Coaching.' *The Journal of Applied Behavioral Science*, 2015. 51(2): pp. 253-276.

20 Morley, K.J., *Gender Balanced Leadership: An Executive Guide*. 2015, Melbourne.

21 Williams, M.J. and L.Z. Tiedens, 'The Subtle Suspension of Backlash: A Meta-Analysis of Penalties for Women's Implicit and Explicit Dominance Behavior.' *Psychological Bulletin*, 2016. 142(2): pp. 165-97.

22 Hoyt, C.L. and S.E. Murphy, 'Managing to Clear the Air: Stereotype Threat, Women, and Leadership.' *The Leadership Quarterly*, 2016. 27(3): pp. 387-399.

23 Sandberg, S. and N. Scovell, *Lean In: Women, Work and the Will to Lead*. 2013, UK: WH Allen.

Chapter 8

1 Crosby, F.J., et al., 'Affirmative Action: Psychological Data and the Policy Debates. *American Psychologist*, 2003. 58(2): pp. 93-115.

2 Rudman, L.A. and P. Glick, *The Social Psychology of Gender*. 2008, New York: The Guilford Press.

3 Chamorro-Premuzic, T., *Why Do So Many Incompetent Men Become Leaders? (And How to Fix It)*. 2019, Boston, Massachusetts: Harvard Business Review Press.

4 Ibid.

5 Ibid.

6 Ibid.

7 Shariatmadari, D., 'Daniel Kahneman: "What Would I Eliminate if I Had a Magic Wand? Overconfidence."', in *The Guardian*. 2015.

8 Chamorro-Premuzic, T., *Why Do So Many Incompetent Men Become Leaders? (And How to Fix It)*. 2019, Boston, Massachusetts: Harvard Business Review Press.

9 Lebowitz, S.. *Why Is It so Hard to Overcome Bias? Because You're Human*. 2016; Available from: www.weforum.org/agenda/2016/11. why-its-so-hard-to-overcome-bias-in-decision-making-according-to-a-psychology-professor.

10 Lehrer, J., 'The Certainty Bias: A Potentially Dangerous Mental Flaw,' in *Scientific American*. 2008.

11 Castilla, E.J. and S. Benard, 'The Paradox of Meritocracy in Organizations.' *Administrative Science Quarterly*, 2010. 55(4): pp. 543-676.

12 Malmström, M., J. Johansson and J. Wincent, 'Gender Stereotypes and Venture Support Decisions: How Governmental Venture Capitalists Socially Construct Entrepreneurs' Potential.' *Entrepreneurship Theory and Practice*, 2017.

13 Kanze, D., et al., 'Male and Female Entrepreneurs Get Asked Different Questions by VCs – and It Affects How Much Funding They Get.' *Harvard Business Review*, 2017 (June 27).

14 Banaji, M.R. and A.G. Greenwald, *Blindspot: Hidden Biases of Good People*. 2013, New York: Delacorte Press.

15 Raina, S., 'Research: The Gender Gap in Startup Success Disappears When Women Fund Women.' *Harvard Business Review*, 2016. July.

16 Mayo, M., 'To Seem Confident Women Have to Be Seen as Warm.' *Harvard Business Review*, 2016. July.

17 Bohnet, I., *What Works: Gender Equality by Design*. 2016, Boston: Harvard University Press.

18 Banaji, M.R. and A.G. Greenwald, *Blindspot: Hidden Biases of Good People*. 2013, New York: Delacorte Press.

19 Priestley, A. *'There Is No Excuse': Salesforce Chief Marc Benioff Was Once in Denial About the Gender Pay Gap, He's Since Spent Millions Closing It*. 2018 [26-1-20]. Available from: www.smartcompany.com.au/people-human-resources/leadership/salesforce-chief-marc-benioff-denial-about-gender-pay-gap-since-spent-millions-closing-it.

20 EnergyAustralia. *Energy Australia Closes Gender Pay Gap*. [cited 2019 8-3-19]. Available from: www.energyaustralia.com.au/about-us/media/news/energyaustralia-closes-gender-pay-gap.

21 Goldin, C. and C. Rouse, 'Orchestrating Impartiality: The Impact of "Blind" Auditions on Female Musicians.' *American Economic Review*, 2000. 90(4): pp. 715-741.

22 Burrell, L., 'We Just Can't Handle Diversity.' *Harvard Business Review*, 2016. July-August: pp. 70-74.
Morse, G., 'Designing a Bias-Free Organization.' *Harvard Business Review*, 2016. July-August: pp. 62-67.

23 Klahre, A.-M. *3 Ways Johnson & Johnson is Taking Talent Acquisition to the Next Level*. 2017 [29-8-17]. Available from: www.jnj.com/innovation/3-ways-johnson-and-johnson-is-taking-talent-acquisition-to-the-next-level.

Part III

1   Male Champions of Change, *Our Progress Report*. 2017: Australia.

Chapter 9

1   Groysberg, B., et al., 'The Leaders' Guide to Corporate Culture.' *Harvard Business Review*, 2018. January-February: pp. 44-52.

2   Coyle, D., *The Culture Code: The Secrets of Highly Successful Groups*. 2018, London: Random House.

3   Groysberg, B., et al., 'The Leaders' Guide to Corporate Culture.' *Harvard Business Review*, 2018. January-February: pp. 44-52.

4   Page, S.E., *The Diversity Bonus*. 2017, US: Princeton University Press.

5   Mackenzie, A., 'BHP Billiton Chief Executive Andrew Mackenzie: Diversity Will Help Fuel Innovation,' in *The Sydney Morning Herald*. 2015.

6   Matos, K., O. O'Neill, and X. Lei, 'Toxic Leadership and the Masculinity Contest Culture: How "Win or Die" Cultures Breed Abusive Leadership.' *Journal of Social Issues*, 2018. 74(3): pp. 500-528.

7   Annunzio, S.L., *Evolutionary Leadership: Dynamic Ways to Make Your Corporate Culture Fast & Flexible*. 2001, USA: Fireside.

8   Ely, R.J. and D.E. Meyerson, 'An Organizational Approach to Undoing Gender: The Unlikely Case of Offshore Oil Platforms.' *Research in Organizational Behavior*, 2010. 30: pp. 3-34.

9   Ibid.

10 Ely, R.J. and M. Kimmel, 'Thoughts on the Workplace as a Masculinity Contest.' *Journal of Social Issues*, 2018. 74(3): pp. 628-634.

11 Annunzio, S.L., *Evolutionary Leadership: Dynamic Ways to Make Your Corporate Culture Fast & Flexible*. 2001, USA: Fireside.

12 Clear, J., *Atomic Habits: Tiny Changes, Remarkable Results*. 2018: Avery.

Part IV

Chapter 10

1   Chugh, D., *The Person You Mean to Be: How Good People Beat Bias*. 2018, New York: HarperBusiness.

2   Chugh, D., *How to Let Go of Being a 'Good' Person and Be a Better Person*. TED@BCG 2018 [26 September 2019]. Available from: www.ted.com/talks/dolly_chugh_how_to_let_go_of_being_

a_good_person_and_become_a_better_person?
language=en#t-339882.

3   Bohnet, I., *What Works: Gender Equality by Design*. 2016, Boston: Harvard University Press.

4   Sharot, T., *The Influential Mind: What the Brain Reveals About Our Power to Change Others*. 2017, United States: Little, Brown.

Chapter 11

1   Amabile, T.M. and S.J. Kramer, 'The Power of Small Wins.' *Harvard Business Review*, 2011. May: pp. 71-80.

2   Morley, K.J. *Leadership Stories That Move Us*. 2016 [21-9-19]. Available from: www.karenmorley.com.au/leadership-stories-that-move-us.

3   Amabile, T.M. and S.J. Kramer, 'The Power of Small Wins.' *Harvard Business Review*, 2011. May: pp. 71-80.

4   Chugh, D., *The Person You Mean to Be: How Good People Beat Bias*. 2018, New York: HarperBusiness.

5   Homan, A.C., et al., 'Bridging Faultlines by Valuing Diversity: Diversity Beliefs, Information Elaboration, and Performance in Diverse Work Groups.' *Journal of Applied Psychology*, 2007. 92(5): pp. 1189-99.

6   Sharot, T., *The Influential Mind: What the Brain Reveals About Our Power to Change Others*. 2017, United States: Little, Brown.

7   Chugh, D., *The Person You Mean to Be: How Good People Beat Bias*. 2018, New York: HarperBusiness.

8   Liswood, L., *The Loudest Duck*. 2009, US: Wiley.

9   Chugh, D., *The Person You Mean to Be: How Good People Beat Bias*. 2018, New York: HarperBusiness.

10   Goleman, D., 'The Focused Leader.' *Harvard Business Review*, 2013. December: pp. 51-59.

11   Sandberg, S. and A. Grant, 'Speaking While Female: Why Women Stay Quiet At Work.' *The New York Times*. 2015: New York.

12   Dennett, H., *Julie Bishop's Days of Allowing Men to Take Credit for Women's Ideas are Over*. 2018 [21-9-19]; February 28 2018. Available from: www.themandarin.com.au/89119-julie-bishop-days-allowing-men-take-credit-womens-ideas-over.

13   Sandberg, S. and A. Grant, 'Speaking While Female: Why Women Stay Quiet At Work.' *The New York Times*. 2015: New York.

14   Woolley, A.W., et al., 'Evidence for a Collective Intelligence Factor in the Performance of Human groups.' *Science*, 2010. 330: pp. 686-688.

Chapter 12

1   Rattan, A., et al. 'Tackling the Underrepresentation of Women in the Media.' *Harvard Business Review*, 2019. June 2019.

2   Australian Human Rights Commission, *Everyone's Business: Fourth National Survey on Sexual Harassment in Australian Workplaces*. 2018, Australian Human Rights Commission.

3   Ibid.

4   Fox, C., 'Is Your Workplace Following the New Rules of #MeToo? Here's the Lowdown.' *Financial Review*. 2018.

5   Rawski, S. *#MeToo, #TimesUp, Now What?* [Video] [cited 2019 25-9-19]. Available from: www.youtube.com/watch?v= Wr89j4zGVRA&feature=youtu.be.

6   Victorian Equal Opportunity & Human Rights Commission, *Independent Review into Sex Discrimination and Sexual Harassment, Including Predatory Behaviour, in Victoria Police*. 2018, Victorian Equal Opportunity & Human Rights Commission.

7   Rudman, L.A. and P. Glick, *The Social Psychology of Gender*. 2008, New York: The Guilford Press.

8   Ibid.

9   Berdahl, J.L., 'The Sexual Harassment of Uppity Women.' *Journal of Applied Psychology*, 2007. 92(2): pp. 425-437.

10 Victorian Equal Opportunity & Human Rights Commission, *Independent Review into Sex Discrimination and Sexual Harassment, Including Predatory Behaviour, in Victoria Police*. 2018, Victorian Equal Opportunity & Human Rights Commission.

Index

Acknowledgements

Like many girls, I read *Little Women* and wanted to be Jo. Her character introduced me to the power and value of independent choice and action. I sincerely want to thank my parents for gifting me this book when I was 10; it had a big impact on me. They also gifted me a wonderful education and, perhaps more importantly, a sense of aspiration. They always expected me to do well, and I therefore expected it of myself. As a consequence of their guidance, I've lived a life of 'ordinary' privilege, and am extremely grateful for it.

While on family, I'd also like to thank my sister and Business Manager Debbie for keeping the business side of things rolling over smoothly while I completed this book.

Nick Marinelli, Ingrid Bakker, Melissa Donald, Chris Sutherland and several anonymous others were generous in their time and support for the stories that appear here. It's such a privilege to work with them and to be able to share their stories so that the book's core principles come to life.

Thanks to Thought Leaders Business School for the deep insights and support. It's such an inspiring and generous community providing tips, suggestions and resources that help me to carve out a writing routine and keep a focus on delivering results. This book was written in half the time of *Lead Like a Coach*!

Major Street's support and guidance has again been second to none. Thanks so much to Lesley, Vanessa, Kerry and all the team for your collaboration in getting the book out to the world.

Contact Karen Morley

Thank you for your interest in *Beat Gender Bias*, and for investing your valuable time to read it.

I sincerely hope that it has provided you with insight, tools and motivation to flex your influence to create greater inclusion. I hope it has helped you to be clearer about what bias is and how it impacts decisions, and that you have a better sense of the most effective action you can take next. If you do, then the book has done its work.

If you want to be an even bigger part of a better world, why not join me in my Inclusionist Quest. We will increase our influence as a supportive, committed community. Let's share the load. Find out more here: www.karenmorley.com.au/inclusionist-quest, or get in touch with me by email at kmorley@ karenmorley.com.au.

Stay tuned for news about follow-up books! Don't hesitate to make a suggestion or recommendation about what you would like to read about – I'd love to write about the diversity and inclusion challenges and insights that you'd like to know more about.

Please stay connected. If you've not already signed up for my newsletters and updates, please do so via my website, www. karenmorley.com.au, where you can also browse through resources and musings on diversity and inclusion. You can also follow me on LinkedIn (au.linkedin.com/in/karenmorley).

Finally, if you'd prefer to discuss your interests or your organisation's needs personally with me, please contact me on +61 438 215 391 or at kmorley@karenmorley.com.au.

www.ingramcontent.com/pod-product-compliance
Lightning Source LLC
Chambersburg PA
CBHW031925190326
41519CB00007B/417